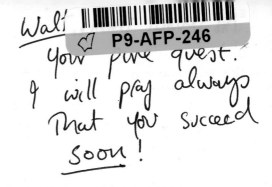

Walt ... your pure quest.
I will pray always
That you succeed
soon!

THE BODHISATTVA VOW

with all my love
Geu Khadro
♡ June 95

Also by Geshe Kelsang Gyatso

Meaningful to Behold
Clear Light of Bliss
Buddhism in the Tibetan Tradition
Heart of Wisdom
Universal Compassion
A Meditation Handbook
Joyful Path of Good Fortune
Guide to Dakini Land

THE BODHISATTVA VOW

THE ESSENTIAL PRACTICES OF
MAHAYANA BUDDHISM

Geshe Kelsang Gyatso

Tharpa Publications
London

First published in 1991

Tharpa Publications
15 Bendemeer Road
London SW15 1JX

Cover painting of The Thirty-five Confession Buddhas
by Ani Kelsang Wangmo
Cover photo of Geshe Kelsang Gyatso by Robin Bath
Line illustrations by Andy Weber

British Library Cataloguing in Publication Data
Gyatso, Geshe Kelsang, 1932–
The Bodhisattva Vow:
The Essential Practices of Mahayana Buddhism
1. Mahayana Buddhism
I. Title
294.3422

ISBN 0 948006 14 5

Set in Palatino by Tharpa Publications
Printed on acid-free 250-year longlife paper
and bound in Great Britain
by Biddles Ltd., Guildford

Contents

Illustrations

Acknowledgements

Our profound thanks go once again to Venerable Geshe Kelsang Gyatso, the author of *The Bodhisattva Vow*, for his inexhaustible great kindness to Dharma students around the world in writing this book. Long may we continue to merit the author's realized and expert guidance along the spiritual path.

Early drafts of the first part of the book were prepared by James Belither from transcripts of the author's original lectures. The main editing work of the entire text was done by Michael Garside, and the final draft was completed by Gelong Thubten Gyatso. Our thanks go to these dedicated students for their kindness, and also to Tsultrim Kelsang and Lucy James who then prepared the completed manuscript for final publication.

Roy Tyson, Director
Manjushri Institute
March 1991

Editorial Note

Because this book is intended as a practical handbook, technical details have been kept to a minimum, and a simplified form of phonetics has been used for rendering Tibetan terms. Many of the practices explained in this book are explained in more detail in *Joyful Path of Good Fortune* and *A Meditation Handbook*.

Buddha Shakyamuni

Introduction

The subject of this book is the Bodhisattva's moral discipline. The Sanskrit term 'Bodhisattva' is the name given to anyone who, motivated by great compassion, has generated bodhichitta, which is a spontaneous wish to attain Buddhahood for the benefit of all living beings. Since everyone has within their mental continuum the seeds of great compassion and bodhichitta, and since everyone can at some time meet a Mahayana[1] Dharma Teacher, it is possible for everyone to become a Bodhisattva by training in Mahayana teachings.

The Bodhisattva's moral discipline is a higher moral discipline and it is the main path that leads to the ultimate happiness of great enlightenment. In general, moral discipline is a virtuous determination to abandon any non-virtuous action. For example, if by seeing the disadvantages of killing, stealing, or sexual misconduct we make a firm decision to refrain from such actions, this is moral discipline. Similarly, the determination to refrain from lying, divisive speech, hurtful speech, idle gossip, covetousness, malice, and holding wrong views is also moral discipline.[2]

In the *Pratimoksha Sutra* Buddha says that it would be better for us to die than to break our moral discipline because death destroys only this one life whereas breaking our moral discipline destroys our opportunity to experience happiness in many future lives and condemns us to experience the sufferings of lower rebirths over and over again.

In Buddhist countries, moral discipline is regarded as very important, and it is for this reason that monks and nuns are held in such high esteem. However, it is not only monks and nuns who need to practise moral discipline. Everyone needs to practise moral discipline because it is the root of all future happiness. Even if we are a very learned scholar, if we ignore the practice of moral discipline our activities will be unsuccessful and we will experience many problems in the future. On the other hand, if we conscientiously observe moral discipline we can solve all our human problems and complete our spiritual practices.

The practice of moral discipline is the main cause of rebirth as a human. If we practise generosity without moral discipline we will experience some good results in the future, but not in a human body. For example, we may be reborn as a pet cat or dog that is well cared for. The reason why some animals receive great care from humans is that they practised generosity in previous lives, but the reason why they have taken a low rebirth is that they broke their moral discipline in previous lives.

If we practise moral discipline by abandoning negative actions such as killing with the motivation to obtain human happiness, this moral discipline will protect us from lower rebirth and cause us to be reborn as a human being in the future. If we practise moral discipline with a sincere wish to attain liberation for ourselves, or full enlightenment for the sake of all sentient beings, this is higher moral discipline. There are three types of higher moral discipline: Pratimoksha moral discipline, Bodhisattva moral discipline, and Tantric moral discipline. These types of moral discipline are distinguished by the motivation with which they are practised and the particular downfalls they abandon. Pratimoksha moral discipline is motivated mainly by the aspiration to attain personal liberation, Bodhisattva moral discipline mainly by bodhichitta, and Tantric moral discipline mainly by special Tantric bodhichitta.[3]

Not every practice of moral discipline entails taking vows. For example, if we realize the many faults of killing and, as a result, make a strong decision to abstain from killing, we are practising moral discipline even though we have not taken a vow. A vow is a virtuous determination to abandon particular faults that is generated in conjunction with a traditional ritual. Just as there are three types of moral discipline, so there are three types of vow: Pratimoksha vows, Bodhisattva vows, and Tantric vows.

'Pratimoksha' means 'personal liberation', and so a Pratimoksha vow is a vow that is motivated mainly by the wish to attain personal liberation. There are eight kinds of Pratimoksha vow:

1 nyennä vows – one-day ordination vows
2 genyenma vows – vows of a laywoman
3 genyenpa vows – vows of a layman
4 getsulma vows – vows of a novice nun
5 getsulpa vows – vows of a novice monk
6 gelobma vows – preliminary vows taken before becoming a fully ordained nun
7 gelongma vows – vows of a fully ordained nun
8 gelongpa vows – vows of a fully ordained monk

The first three are lay vows and the remaining five are ordination vows. Buddha gave extensive instructions on the Pratimoksha moral discipline and the Pratimoksha vows in the *Vinaya Sutras*.[4]

This book is concerned principally with the Bodhisattva vows. In *Guide to the Bodhisattva's Way of Life*, Shantideva advises those who want to know about the Bodhisattva vows first to study the *Akashagarbha Sutra*, and then, for a more detailed explanation of the daily practices of a Bodhisattva, to read the *Compendium of*

Trainings. Shantideva explains that those who have taken Bodhisattva vows should know what the root and secondary downfalls are, how to prevent the vows from degenerating, how to purify downfalls, and how to complete the practice of the Bodhisattva vows. All these are explained in this book.

Once we have taken Bodhisattva vows we should strive to prevent them from degenerating by retaking our vows several times each day, and then avoid incurring root or secondary downfalls by relying on mindfulness, alertness, and conscientiousness.

There are four main causes of the degeneration of the Pratimoksha, Bodhisattva, or Tantric vows, which are known as 'the four doors of receiving downfalls'. They are: not knowing what the downfalls are, not respecting Buddha's instructions, developing strong delusions, and lacking conscientiousness.

To close the first door we should learn what the downfalls are and how they are incurred. This can be done by listening to teachings on the subject or by reading authentic commentaries such as the instructions given in the next section.

To close the second door we should try to overcome disrespect by contemplating the following:

Since Buddha is omniscient, knowing all past, present, and future phenomena simultaneously and directly, and since he has great compassion for all living beings without exception, there is no valid reason for developing disrespect towards his teachings. It is only due to ignorance that I sometimes disbelieve them.

To close the third door we should try to subdue our strong delusions by practising the meditations described in *A Meditation Handbook.* If, by practising Lamrim,[5] we are able always to maintain good intentions such as love, compassion, and bodhichitta, there will be no basis for incurring Pratimoksha or Bodhisattva downfalls, and if, by practising generation and completion stages, we overcome ordinary appearances and ordinary conceptions,[6] there will be no basis for incurring Tantric downfalls.

We can close the fourth door, lacking conscientiousness, by repeatedly bringing to mind the disadvantages of committing downfalls and the advantages of pure moral discipline. In this way we become more conscientious.

In brief, the method for preventing our vows from degenerating is to train in renunciation, bodhichitta, the correct view of emptiness, generation stage, and completion stage. By sincerely practising these we overcome our ordinary attitudes and control our mind, thereby removing any basis for downfalls.

Complete Subduer with the Essence of Vajra

Taking the Bodhisattva Vows

There now follows an explanation of the methods for receiving and maintaining the Bodhisattva vows, and for completing the vows and trainings of a Bodhisattva.

THE METHOD FOR RECEIVING AND MAINTAINING THE BODHISATTVA VOWS

The main purpose of practising the Mahayana is to attain Buddhahood to benefit all sentient beings. To accomplish this aim we must first generate bodhichitta and then adopt the Bodhisattva's way of life by taking and keeping the Bodhisattva vows.

The bodhichitta that we generate before taking the Bodhisattva vows is called 'aspiring bodhichitta'. This is a mind that aspires to attain enlightenment for the benefit of others but does not yet engage in the actual practices of the Bodhisattva's training. It is like someone intending to go to India but not yet setting out on the journey. After we have taken the Bodhisattva vows our bodhichitta transforms into engaging bodhichitta. This is a mind that actually engages in the practices that lead to the final destination of Buddhahood.

We must first receive the Bodhisattva vows from a qualified Spiritual Guide. Once we have received them at such a ceremony we can take them on our own at any time and as often as we wish. When we do so, we visualize the Field for Accumulating Merit in front of us and repeat three times the promise to keep the moral discipline of a Bodhisattva and to avoid all downfalls by engaging in the practice of the six perfections. We can renew or strengthen this promise by engaging in the following practice.

Taking refuge vows

We begin by considering the benefits of going for refuge:

1 *We become a pure Buddhist*
2 *We establish the foundation for taking all other vows*
3 *We purify the negative karma that we have accumulated in the past*
4 *We daily accumulate a vast collection of merit* [7]
5 *We are held back from falling into the lower realms*
6 *We are protected from harm inflicted by humans and non-humans*
7 *We fulfil all our temporary and ultimate wishes*
8 *We quickly attain the full enlightenment of Buddhahood*

Through contemplating these benefits we make a strong determination or promise to go for refuge to the Three Jewels[8] until we attain enlightenment. We then recite the following prayer three times:

I and all sentient beings, until we achieve enlightenment,
Go for refuge to Buddha, Dharma, and Sangha.

This is like a pure container into which we now put the nectar of the Bodhisattva vows.

Generating bodhichitta

We begin by considering the benefits of bodhichitta:

1 *We enter the gateway to the Mahayana*
2 *We become a Son or Daughter of the Buddhas* [9]

3 *We surpass Hearers and Solitary Conquerors*[10]

4 *We become worthy to receive offerings and prostrations from humans and gods*

5 *We easily create a vast amount of merit*

6 *We quickly destroy powerful negativities*

7 *We fulfil all our wishes*

8 *We are free from harm by spirits and so forth*

9 *We accomplish all the spiritual grounds and paths*

10 *We have a state of mind that is the source of peace and happiness for all beings*

Through contemplating these benefits we make a strong determination or promise to attain Buddhahood for the benefit of all living beings. While concentrating on this determination we recite the following prayer three times:

Through the virtues I collect by giving and other perfections,
May I become a Buddha for the benefit of all.

Maintaining aspiring bodhichitta by means of ritual

To prevent our bodhichitta from degenerating we make the following promise three times:

From this time forth until I become a Buddha,
I shall keep even at the cost of my life
A mind wishing to attain complete enlightenment
To free all living beings from the fears of cyclic
   existence and solitary peace.[11]

In this way we undertake to observe the eight precepts of aspiring bodhichitta. These can be found in Appendix II.

Taking the Bodhisattva vows

Only by engaging in the Bodhisattva's trainings, the practice of the six perfections, and by avoiding the root and secondary downfalls of the Bodhisattva vows can we fulfil the two aims of our bodhichitta – to attain Buddhahood ourselves and to lead all other beings to that state of ultimate happiness. Realizing this, we make a strong determination or promise to engage in the practice of the six perfections and to avoid the root and secondary downfalls. While concentrating on this promise, we recite the following ritual prayer three times:

O Gurus, Buddhas, and Bodhisattvas
Please listen to what I now say.
Just as all the previous Sugatas [12]
Generated the mind of enlightenment
And accomplished all the stages
Of the Bodhisattva training,
So will I too for the sake of all beings
Generate the mind of enlightenment
And accomplish all the stages
Of the Bodhisattva training.

Maintaining joy and conscientiousness

So that we may complete our practice of the Bodhisattva vows, we generate and maintain a feeling of joy and conscientiousness while reciting the following two verses:

Now my life has borne great fruit,
My human life has attained great meaning;
Today I am born into the lineage of Buddha
And have become a Bodhisattva.

All my actions from now on
Shall accord with this noble lineage;
And upon this lineage, pure and faultless,
I shall never bring disgrace.

Taking refuge in the Three Jewels and keeping the commitments of refuge are the foundation of the Bodhisattva vows, and refraining from the root and secondary downfalls is the actual practice of the Bodhisattva vows.

Jewel of Radiant Light

The Downfalls of the Bodhisattva Vows

THE METHOD FOR COMPLETING THE VOWS AND TRAININGS OF A BODHISATTVA

By taking the Bodhisattva vows we promise to engage in the trainings of a Bodhisattva, all of which are included in the practice of the six perfections. The six perfections are the highway to enlightenment and the downfalls of the Bodhisattva vows are the principal obstacles along the way. Therefore, now that we have taken the vows, we need to emphasize two main practices: to avoid the downfalls of the Bodhisattva vows and to practise the six perfections. These practices will now be explained under the following three headings:

1 An explanation of the downfalls of the Bodhisattva vows
2 A method for purifying downfalls
3 The actual trainings of a Bodhisattva

An explanation of the downfalls of the Bodhisattva vows

The instructions on the downfalls of the Bodhisattva vows include extensive advice on how we should conduct our daily lives by transforming all our actions into the Bodhisattva's way of life. These instructions are extremely important for those who have taken the Bodhisattva vows. By putting them into practice we shall gradually complete the Bodhisattva's training and eventually attain the supreme bliss of Buddhahood.

There are forty-six secondary downfalls and eighteen root downfalls. These will now be explained in detail.

The forty-six secondary downfalls

If we commit any of the following secondary downfalls we damage our Bodhisattva vows but we do not actually break them; just as a small knock may crack, but not break, a cup.

1 Not making offerings to the Three Jewels every day By taking the Bodhisattva vows we commit ourselves to making offerings to the Three Jewels every day. These can be physical offerings, such as material gifts or gestures of respect; verbal offerings, such as praises; or mental offerings of faith. If a day passes without our making any of these three kinds of offering we incur a secondary downfall. This commitment advises us that we need to accumulate merit every day by making physical, verbal, or mental offerings to the Three Jewels.

2 Indulging in worldly pleasures out of attachment Whenever we enjoy pleasures such as food, drink, clothing, or music, we should try to do so while maintaining bodhichitta motivation. If we fail to do this and indulge in such pleasures simply out of attachment or discontent we incur a secondary downfall. This commitment advises us that we should transform our daily activities into the Bodhisattva's way of life by continuously maintaining bodhichitta motivation.

3 Being disrespectful to those who received Bodhisattva vows before us By showing disrespect to a practitioner who received Bodhisattva vows before us we incur a secondary downfall. This commitment advises us that we need to respect senior Bodhisattva Sangha in order to increase our merit.

4 Not replying to others If someone greets us in a friendly and courteous manner and, without a good reason, we give no reply we incur a secondary downfall. This commitment advises us that we should try to make others' minds happy by giving suitable answers and advice.

5 Not accepting invitations If someone with a good motivation invites us to dinner, to a party, or for an outing and, without a good reason, we decline merely out of pride, laziness, or anger we incur a secondary downfall. Valid reasons for declining invitations are: we are sick, we do not have the free time, it would make others unhappy, there would be a danger or obstacle to our Dharma practice, etc. This commitment advises us that in accepting invitations, we should make a dedication prayer that the host's generosity becomes a cause for all living beings to experience the enjoyments of a Buddha.

6 Not accepting gifts If we are given gold, money, or other gifts and, without a good reason, we refuse them merely out of pride, anger, or laziness we incur a secondary downfall. This commitment advises us that in accepting offerings from others we should use them in the most meaningful way.

7 Not giving Dharma to those who desire it If someone with a sincere desire to practise Dharma requests us to teach them and, without a good reason, we refuse merely out of laziness we incur a secondary downfall. Valid reasons for not teaching include: we do not know the subject well enough, it is not suitable to teach them, others will be unhappy, we are ill, we do not have the free time, and so on. This commitment advises us that whenever we have the chance we should try to eliminate the

Powerful King of the Nagas

darkness of ignorance from the minds of others by giving Dharma teachings.

8 Forsaking those who have broken their moral discipline We incur a secondary downfall if we ignore with a judgmental or self-righteous attitude those who have broken their moral discipline. This commitment advises us that we should keep the intention to help all living beings, including those who have broken their moral discipline.

9 Not acting in ways that cause others to generate faith To help others effectively it is necessary to conduct ourselves in a way that causes them to develop confidence in us. If we fail to do this but retain bad habits that are likely to attract criticism, such as drinking or smoking, we incur a secondary downfall. This commitment advises us that we should keep pure discipline sincerely and show a good example so as to increase others' faith in us. In this way they will derive great results from our teachings.

10 Doing little to benefit others An austere, solitary lifestyle is appropriate for Hinayanists because their principal objective is to renounce attachment and thereby achieve their own liberation. However, a Mahayanist should not needlessly diminish his or her capacity to help others by shunning wealth, reputation, or involvement with other people. If we do this without a special, altruistic motivation we incur a secondary downfall. This commitment advises us that if we have bodhichitta motivation we can increase our wealth and reputation providing we use it solely to bring increased benefit to sentient beings.

11 Not believing that Bodhisattvas' compassion ensures that all their actions are pure Buddha taught that since higher Bodhisattvas have abandoned self-cherishing[13] and are motivated only by compassion, all their actions, even killing, stealing, and so forth, are free from negativity. If we refuse to believe this we incur a secondary downfall. This commitment advises us that we should rejoice in all Bodhisattvas' actions and that we too should be motivated solely by compassion and bodhichitta.

As with the preceding eleven secondary downfalls, each of the remaining thirty-five carries with it some special advice. Although the advice relating to the remaining downfalls is not explicitly indicated below, we should try to understand what it is as we contemplate each downfall.

12 Acquiring wealth or fame through wrong livelihood
Some people, desirous of wealth, praise, respect, and so forth, resort to dishonest means to acquire it. They pretend to be special, holy people, outwardly showing good behaviour, talking smoothly, flattering others, praising the possessions of others while subtly hinting that they need such things themselves, or giving small presents in the hope of receiving larger presents in return. If, with selfish motives, we behave in such a way we incur a secondary downfall.

13 Indulging in frivolity   If, without a good reason but motivated only by excitement, attachment, or a lack of conscientiousness, we indulge in frivolous activities such as singing, dancing, playing, or meaningless conversation we incur a secondary downfall.

14 Claiming that Bodhisattvas need not abandon samsara
Some people, misunderstanding what samsara is, assert that Bodhisattvas need not abandon samsara or delusions,[14] but can attain enlightenment in the midst of samsara while working for the welfare of sentient beings. If we hold this view and encourage others to think the same we incur a secondary downfall because such views interfere with our spiritual progress.

15 Not avoiding a bad reputation If we unnecessarily engage in actions that cause us to receive criticism or a bad reputation we incur a secondary downfall. However, if our actions benefit many beings, cause the pure Buddhadharma to flourish, or are necessary to preserve the integrity of our moral discipline, it does not matter if a few people criticize us.

16 Not helping others to avoid negativity If we have the ability and the opportunity to help someone avoid committing negative actions but, without a good reason, fail to do so we incur a secondary downfall.

17 Retaliating to harm or abuse If out of impatience we repay abuse with abuse, beating with beating, criticism with criticism, and so on we incur a secondary downfall.

18 Not apologizing when we have the opportunity If we have disturbed another person by acting in an unskilful way and later the opportunity to apologize arises but, out of pride or laziness, we fail to do so we incur a secondary downfall.

19 Not accepting others' apologies If someone who has previously harmed us later apologizes and, without a good reason but not out of resentment, we refuse to accept their apology we incur a secondary downfall. If we do so out of resentment we incur a root downfall.

20 Making no effort to control our anger Sometimes, because of strong habits of anger or because of difficult circumstances, we find ourselves getting angry. If at such times we do not make a special effort to practise patience we incur a secondary downfall.

21 Gathering a circle of followers out of desire for profit or respect If, for selfish reasons, we try to gather students, disciples, or followers we incur a secondary downfall.

Leader of the Heroes

22 Not trying to overcome laziness   We have promised to attain Buddhahood for the sake of all sentient beings, but to accomplish this requires great effort. If we do not try to eliminate our laziness, or our attachment to sleep and other worldly pleasures, we incur a secondary downfall.

23 Indulging in senseless conversation out of attachment   If we spend much of our time doing this we incur a secondary downfall.

24 Neglecting to train in mental stabilization   The attainment of tranquil abiding is essential if we wish to achieve profound realizations. If we fail to make an effort to listen to and think about the instructions on tranquil abiding, or to improve our concentration by training in tranquil abiding, we incur a secondary downfall.

25 Not overcoming obstacles to mental stabilization   In this context there are five obstacles to mental stabilization or concentration:

1 Needless self-reproach and excitement
2 Malicious thoughts
3 Sleep and dullness
4 Distracting desires
5 Frequent and disturbing doubts

If we make no effort to abandon these we incur a secondary downfall.

26 Being preoccupied with the taste of mental stabilization Here, the 'taste' of mental stabilization is the experience of bliss, peace, and suppleness induced by concentration. If we become attached to this and regard it as the ultimate result of concentration we incur a downfall because this attachment diminishes our wish to help others and hinders our Mahayana practice. The real value of concentration is not the temporary bliss that it induces but its being the means by which higher realizations can be achieved.

27 Abandoning the Hinayana The teachings and practices of the Hinayana are methods to release beings from the sufferings of samsara; therefore they are holy Dharma and objects to be respected. If we regard them as contradictory to the Mahayana and believe that they must be abandoned we incur a secondary downfall.

28 Studying the Hinayana to the detriment of our Mahayana practice To attain bodhichitta and other Mahayana realizations, and finally to accomplish the state of Buddhahood, we need to study and practise the Mahayana teachings. If instead of doing this we put great effort into studying the Hinayana with the result that our Mahayana practice is weakened we incur a secondary downfall.

29 Studying non-Dharma subjects without a good reason If we study non-Dharma subjects so as to increase our capacity to help other beings this will not interfere with our Mahayana practice, but if we study non-Dharma subjects without a good reason we incur a secondary downfall.

30 Becoming engrossed in non-Dharma subjects for their own sake Sometimes we may begin to study non-Dharma subjects for good reasons but gradually become so engrossed in them that we lose sight of our original intentions and end up studying them simply for pleasure. The result of this is likely to be that we will lose the energy we have for Dharma study and practice. If we allow this to happen we incur a secondary downfall. This downfall applies as much to the study of academic non-Dharma subjects as it does to more practical subjects.

31 Criticizing other Mahayana traditions Within the Mahayana there is a great variety of different traditions, and each tradition has its own texts and practices. If some of these appear to be contrary to our own tradition we should not discriminate against them or criticize them without a good reason. If we do so with a deluded motivation we incur a secondary downfall.

32 Praising ourself and scorning others This is similar to the first root downfall except that here we are motivated by slight pride but have no intention to deceive others.

33 Making no effort to study Dharma Listening to Dharma teachings and reading Dharma books are the lamps that dispel the darkness of ignorance. If, without a good reason, we make no effort to do either we incur a secondary downfall.

34 Preferring to rely on books rather than on our Spiritual Guide The root of Dharma realizations is sincere reliance on our Spiritual Guide. If we neglect this practice and prefer to acquire our understanding from books we incur a secondary downfall.

35 Not going to the assistance of those in need If someone asks for our help, or we realize that they hope for it, and we are in a position to help them and yet, out of laziness or some other delusion, we do not go to their assistance we incur a secondary downfall. For example, if someone asks to be shown the way, or asks for practical or spiritual help, or requests us to mediate in a dispute, we should assist in whatever way we can.

36 Neglecting to take care of the sick If we show no concern for sick people or animals whom we encounter and do not do our best to help them we incur a secondary downfall.

37 Not acting to dispel suffering Whenever we see humans who are physically or mentally handicapped, or insane, or whenever we see animals, we should feel compassion and consider how we can help them. If we are

Glorious Pleasure

unable to be of any practical assistance, we should at least pray for them. If we do nothing we incur a secondary downfall.

38 Not helping others to overcome their bad habits If there are people who habitually engage in behaviour that directly or indirectly harms themselves or others and we have the opportunity skilfully to help them overcome these habits, we should do so. If we cannot help them directly we should at least pray for them. If we do nothing we incur a secondary downfall. This downfall differs from the sixteenth secondary downfall in that the former concerns specific, heavy negative actions, whereas this one concerns frequently repeated, but otherwise relatively minor, unskilful actions such as smoking, drinking, petty theft, or acting in ways that cause disharmony.

39 Not returning help to those who benefit us We should always remember the kindness of those who benefit us and maintain the intention to repay them. If we completely forget their kindness we incur a secondary downfall.

40 Not relieving the distress of others If we meet people who are beset with grief and have the opportunity to comfort them and yet do nothing we incur a secondary downfall.

41 Not giving to those who seek charity When beggars or others in need of our charity approach us we must try to give them something. If we refuse for some invalid reason other than miserliness we incur a secondary downfall. If we refuse out of miserliness we incur a root downfall.

42 Not taking special care of disciples If we have disciples we must help them by guiding them along the spiritual path and, as far as we are able to, provide them with whatever they need for their Dharma practice. If we do not take special care of our faithful disciples we incur a secondary downfall.

43 Not acting in accordance with the inclinations of others When relating to others we should try to please them by conforming with their wishes whenever possible, unless of course their wishes are wrong and would lead to great suffering. If we ignore the wishes of others without a good reason we incur a secondary downfall.

44 Not praising the good qualities of others If we see someone whose conduct is a good example for our Dharma practice we should rejoice in their good qualities and praise them. If, motivated by envy, pride, jealousy, or some other delusion, we do not praise them we incur a secondary downfall.

45 Not doing wrathful actions when appropriate There are times when it is necessary to resort to wrathful methods, such as speaking in a very forceful manner, to prevent someone committing negative actions, or to subdue their pride. If we realize clearly that such a time has come, and we know that our wrathful action will greatly benefit them in the future, we incur a secondary downfall if for some incorrect reason we do not carry out that action.

46 Not using miracle powers, threatening actions, and so forth When we perform wrathful actions we should use whatever miracle powers we have, otherwise we will incur a secondary downfall. However, many realized Masters, such as Je Tsongkhapa, have said that the time for using miracle powers has now passed because these days people are likely to think that we are engaging in black magic, with the result that Buddhadharma will be brought into disrepute and our own safety may be threatened. Therefore, we should follow the example of the Kadampa Geshes such as Dromtönpa, Geshe Potawa, and

Je Tsongkhapa. Though they possessed potent miracle powers they never displayed them. Outwardly they always remained like ordinary people, never claiming to be in any way special. They lived among ordinary people and helped them principally by encouraging them to cultivate love, compassion, and bodhichitta, and by teaching them all the stages of the path to enlightenment. Nowadays this is the most useful way for Bodhisattvas to act.

The eighteen root downfalls

The root downfalls are more serious than the secondary downfalls because if we incur a root downfall we actually break our Bodhisattva vows, whereas if we incur a secondary downfall we damage our vows but we do not completely break them.

Altogether, there are eighteen root downfalls, which are explained in *The Bodhisattvas' Grounds* by Asanga and *Compendium of Trainings* by Shantideva. Although only eighteen are enumerated, each root downfall has many different aspects.

1 Praising ourself and scorning others　We incur a root downfall if we praise ourself with the motivation of deceiving others so that we might receive gifts or enhance our reputation. We also incur a root downfall if we criticize others with the wish to hurt them. In both cases, the downfall is complete only if someone hears and understands our words.

2 Not giving wealth or Dharma　If someone asks us to give material help such as financial assistance, or spiritual help such as teachings or Dharma books, and we are in a position to oblige but out of miserliness refuse we incur a root downfall.

Jewel Fire

3 Not accepting others' apologies   If someone who has physically or verbally harmed us later apologizes and we refuse to accept their apology, preferring to harbour a grudge, we incur a root downfall.

4 Abandoning the Mahayana   If we reject any Mahayana scripture that teaches either the vast or the profound path,[15] claiming that it is not Buddha's teaching, we incur a root downfall. It is also a downfall to propagate views that contradict the Dharma and to encourage others to practise such false teachings.

5 Stealing the property of the Three Jewels   We incur a root downfall if we steal anything that has been offered to the Three Jewels.

6 Abandoning Dharma   We incur this downfall if we criticize any of Buddha's Hinayana or Mahayana teachings, declaring that they are not Buddhadharma and therefore should not be practised.

7 Taking away saffron robes   This downfall can be incurred only by those in positions of power in monastic communities. Should such people, with a bad motivation, expel monks or nuns from the monastery by taking back their robes they incur a root downfall, even if those whom they expel have previously broken their ordination vows.

8 Committing the five heinous actions   These actions are killing one's father, killing one's mother, killing a Foe Destroyer, maliciously wounding a Buddha, and causing a schism within the Sangha.

9 Holding wrong views   We incur a root downfall if we hold wrong views denying the law of karma, the existence of past and future lives, or other truths that we need to believe in order to achieve liberation.

10 Destroying places such as towns   We incur a root downfall if, with a bad motivation, we wilfully destroy a place of habitation or an environment.

11 **Explaining emptiness to those who are likely to mis-understand**   We incur a root downfall if we teach emptiness[16] in an unskilful way and cause those who are listening to develop serious and harmful misunderstandings.

12 Causing others to abandon the Mahayana   If we cause Mahayana practitioners to give up their bodhichitta by telling them that they will never become a Buddha because the practice of the six perfections is beyond their capacity, and advise them to enter the less demanding Hinayana path by which liberation is swiftly attained, we incur a root downfall.

13 Causing others to abandon the Pratimoksha   We incur a root downfall if we cause an ordained person to give up their Vinaya practice by saying that the Vinaya is a Hinayana practice that is not relevant to the Mahayana path.

14 Belittling the Hinayana   We incur a root downfall if we have a disrespectful opinion of the Hinayana path, maintaining that it does not lead to actual liberation.

15 Speaking falsely about profound emptiness   If we lack a correct understanding of emptiness and yet teach emptiness to others, claiming with a selfish motivation that we have a direct realization of emptiness, we incur a root downfall.

16 Accepting property that has been stolen from the Three Jewels   We incur this downfall if we accept goods that we know to have been stolen from the Three Jewels. For example, some money may have been offered to a Dharma community for a puja or for the publication of Dharma books. If someone appropriates this money and then offers a portion of it to us, and we accept with full knowledge that it has been stolen, we incur a root downfall.

17 Making bad rules Those in charge of spiritual communities incur this downfall if they make rules that unnecessarily interfere with pure Dharma practice, for example by organizing the community in such a way that business activities take precedence over the practice of meditation.

18 Giving up bodhichitta If, due to self-cherishing or discouragement, we give up our bodhichitta motivation we incur a root downfall and destroy the foundation of our Mahayana realizations.

To incur a root downfall four binding factors must be present:

  1 Not regarding the action as wrong
  2 Not wishing to abstain from the action in the future
  3 Rejoicing in the action
  4 Having no sense of shame or consideration for others[17]

For example, if we praise ourself in the hope of deceiving others into giving us money we create the action of the first root downfall, but if we immediately recognize that we have done wrong we will not incur the actual root downfall. Likewise, if we immediately regret the action, feel ashamed or embarrassed by it, or develop the intention never to repeat it, the complete downfall will not be incurred. This applies to all the other root downfalls except the ninth and the eighteenth. To incur these downfalls it is not necessary for the four binding factors to be present; just by adopting wrong views or giving up bodhichitta we incur a root downfall.

To avoid incurring the root and secondary downfalls it is essential to know what they are; therefore as soon as we have taken the Bodhisattva vows we should make a determined effort to learn them and commit them to memory. We should try to understand each downfall, think about how we might come to incur it, and make plans to avoid such situations.

It is important to be skilful in our approach to the vows. We should not have unrealistic expectations or make promises that we cannot keep. Instead, we should adopt the Bodhisattva's way of life gradually. Each of the vows can be kept on many levels. For example, we have a vow to abandon the obstacles to developing concentration, but it is impossible to abandon all these obstacles at once. First we should try to avoid gross distractions and then gradually strive to abandon the subtle interferences. All the Bodhisattva vows are aspects of the practice of the six perfections. Until we attain enlightenment we need continually to improve our practice of the six perfections and, in this way, gradually deepen the level at which we are able to keep the vows.

When a Teacher gives Bodhisattva vows he should explain them well. He should not encourage his disciples to promise to keep all the vows perfectly from the start. Moreover, from their side, the disciples should not make over-enthusiastic promises, pledging to keep all the vows faultlessly without even knowing what they are. Such disciples will break their vows the very next day. After taking Bodhisattva vows an intelligent disciple will first learn what they involve, then he will resolve to keep each one to the best of his ability and gradually improve his practice of the Bodhisattva moral discipline.

The advice to keep the vows gradually does not mean that we can temporarily put to one side the vows that we do not like. We have to work with all the vows, gradually improving the way we observe them. For example, as our miserliness decreases we will be able to keep the vows relating to giving more purely, and as our anger decreases we will be able to keep those concerned with patience more purely. Thus, we should begin to practise all the vows as soon as we have taken them, practise to the best of our ability, and never lose the determination to keep the vows perfectly in the future.

Jewel Moonlight

A Method for Purifying Downfalls

In our previous lives, while under the influence of deluded minds, we created a great deal of negative karma, and we also transgressed our commitments and incurred root and secondary downfalls. As a result we now experience difficulties in developing faith and conviction in Dharma and in making progress on the stages of the path to enlightenment. Since these transgressions and downfalls seriously obstruct our spiritual development, it is essential that we purify them.

In *Akashagharba Sutra*, Buddha says that those who have incurred root downfalls of the Bodhisattva vows should generate strong regret and, at the dawn of each day, face east and sincerely make offerings and prostrations to the Bodhisattva Akashagharba while reciting his name. That Bodhisattva will then appear in various aspects, either directly in front of the practitioner or in his or her dreams. Akashagharba will then purify their downfalls and the practitioner will achieve powerful concentration and a strong realization of mindfulness.

One of the best methods for purifying downfalls, however, is recommended by Shantideva in *Guide to the Bodhisattva's Way of Life*, where he advises us:

Three times during the day and the night
You should recite the *Three Heaps*,
And, in dependence upon the Conquerors and
bodhichitta,
Purify any downfalls that remain.

Meaningful to Behold

Here, the *'Three Heaps'* refers to the *Mahayana Sutra of the Three Superior Heaps*, or *The Bodhisattva's Confession of Moral Downfalls*, the root text of which now follows.

THE MAHAYANA SUTRA OF THE THREE SUPERIOR HEAPS

Namo: The Bodhisattva's Confession of Moral Downfalls

I, whose name is . . . , at all times go for refuge to the Guru, go for refuge to the Buddha, go for refuge to the Dharma, go for refuge to the Sangha.

To the Teacher, Blessed One, Tathagata, Foe Destroyer, Completely Perfect Buddha, Glorious Conqueror Shakyamuni I prostrate.

To the Tathagata Complete Subduer with the Essence of Vajra I prostrate.

To the Tathagata Jewel of Radiant Light I prostrate.

To the Tathagata Powerful King of the Nagas I prostrate.

To the Tathagata Leader of the Heroes I prostrate.

To the Tathagata Glorious Pleasure I prostrate.

To the Tathagata Jewel Fire I prostrate.

To the Tathagata Jewel Moonlight I prostrate.

To the Tathagata Meaningful to Behold I prostrate.

To the Tathagata Jewel Moon I prostrate.

To the Tathagata Stainless One I prostrate.

To the Tathagata Bestower of Glory I prostrate.

To the Tathagata Pure One I prostrate.

To the Tathagata Transforming with Purity I prostrate.

Jewel Moon

To the Tathagata Water Deity I prostrate.

To the Tathagata God of Water Deities I prostrate.

To the Tathagata Glorious Excellence I prostrate.

To the Tathagata Glorious Sandalwood I prostrate.

To the Tathagata Endless Splendour I prostrate.

To the Tathagata Glorious Light I prostrate.

To the Tathagata Glorious One without Sorrow I prostrate.

To the Tathagata Son without Craving I prostrate.

To the Tathagata Glorious Flower I prostrate.

To the Tathagata Clearly Knowing through Enjoying Pure Radiance I prostrate.

To the Tathagata Clearly Knowing through Enjoying Lotus Radiance I prostrate.

To the Tathagata Glorious Wealth I prostrate.

To the Tathagata Glorious Mindfulness I prostrate.

To the Tathagata Glorious Name of Great Renown I prostrate.

To the Tathagata King of the Victory Banner Head of the Powerful Ones I prostrate.

To the Tathagata Glorious One Complete Subduer I prostrate.

To the Tathagata Great Victor in Battle I prostrate.

To the Tathagata Glorious One Complete Subduer Passed Beyond I prostrate.

To the Tathagata Glorious Array Illuminating All I prostrate.

Stainless One

To the Tathagata Jewel Lotus Great Subduer I prostrate.

To the Tathagata Foe Destroyer, Completely Perfect
   Buddha, King of Mount Meru Seated Firmly on a
   Jewel and a Lotus I prostrate.

O all you [Tathagatas] and all the others, however many
Tathagatas, the Foe Destroyers, the Completely Perfect
Buddhas, the Blessed Ones there are dwelling and abid-
ing in all the worldly realms of the ten directions, all you
Buddhas, the Blessed Ones, please listen to me.

In this life and in all my lives since beginningless time,
in all my places of rebirth whilst wandering in cyclic
existence, I have done negative actions, have ordered
them to be done, and have rejoiced in their being done. I
have stolen the property of the bases of offering, the
property of the Sangha, and the property of the Sanghas
of the ten directions, have ordered it to be stolen, and
have rejoiced in it being stolen. I have committed the five
unbounded heinous actions, have ordered them to be
committed, and have rejoiced in their being committed. I
have completely engaged in the paths of the ten non-
virtuous actions, have ordered others to engage in them,
and have rejoiced in their engaging in them.

Being obstructed by such karmic obstructions, I shall
become a hell being, or I shall be born as an animal, or I
shall go to the land of the hungry ghosts, or I shall be
born as a barbarian in an irreligious country, or I shall be
born as a long-life god, or I shall come to have incomplete
senses, or I shall come to hold wrong views, or I shall
have no opportunity to please a Buddha.

All such karmic obstructions I declare in the presence of
the Buddhas, the Blessed Ones, who have become exalted
wisdom, who have become 'eyes', who have become witnesses, who have become valid, who see with their wisdom.
I confess without concealing or hiding anything, and from
now on I shall avoid and refrain from such actions.

Bestower of Glory

All you Buddhas, the Blessed Ones, please listen to me. In this life and in all my previous lives since beginningless time, in all my places of rebirth whilst wandering in cyclic existence, whatever root of virtue there is in my giving to others, even in my giving a morsel of food to one born as an animal; whatever root of virtue there is in my maintaining moral discipline; whatever root of virtue there is in my actions conducive to great liberation; whatever root of virtue there is in my acting to fully ripen sentient beings; whatever root of virtue there is in my generating a supreme mind of enlightenment; and whatever root of virtue there is in my unsurpassed exalted wisdom; all of these assembled, gathered, and collected together, by fully dedicating them to the unsurpassed, to that of which there is no higher, to that which is even higher than the high, and to that which surpasses the unsurpassed, I fully dedicate to the unsurpassed, perfect, complete enlightenment.

Just as the Buddhas, the Blessed Ones of the past, have dedicated fully, just as the Buddhas, the Blessed Ones who are yet to come, will dedicate fully, and just as the Buddhas, the Blessed Ones who are living now, dedicate fully, so too do I dedicate fully.

I confess individually all negative actions. I rejoice in all merit. I beseech and request all the Buddhas. May I attain the holy, supreme, unsurpassed, exalted wisdom.

Whoever are the Conquerors, the supreme beings living now, those of the past, and likewise those who are yet to come, with a boundless ocean of praise for all your good qualities, and with my palms pressed together I go close to you for refuge.

This concludes the Mahayana Sutra entitled the *Sutra of the Three Superior Heaps.*

Pure One

AN EXPLANATION OF THE PRACTICE

This has three parts:

1 An introduction to the practice
2 The visualization
3 The actual practice

An introduction to the practice

This Sutra is included within the *Collection of Precious Jewels Sutra* (Tib. könchog tsegpa). It is called the *Sutra of the Three Superior Heaps* because it contains three 'heaps' or collections of virtue: prostration, purification, and dedication.

In this practice we visualize the Thirty-five Confession Buddhas and practise purification in their presence. In general, all Buddhas have the power to protect sentient beings from suffering and negative karma but, because of the prayers and dedications they made while they were Bodhisattvas, these Thirty-five Buddhas have a special karmic link with the humans of this world. Through the power of their blessings and prayers we can swiftly purify even the heaviest negative actions simply by faithfully reciting their names.

Any sentient being, even a worm or an insect, can commit negative actions, but only humans have the fortune to be able to purify them. We have been accumulating non-virtuous actions and experiencing their suffering results since beginningless time, but we now have the opportunity to purify them completely. We should make use of this precious opportunity to purify our negative karma, not to create more! Since purification is the root of future happiness and spiritual realizations we should strive to cleanse our mind of delusions and negative karma by engaging in the practice of the *Sutra of the Three Superior Heaps*.

Transforming with Purity

Merely beholding Buddha's body or representations of his body or mind is immensely beneficial. There are many true stories that illustrate this. Once, at Nalanda Monastery,[18] Chandrakirti developed a strong wish to meet Buddha Avalokiteshvara[19] and so he made fervent requests day and night. Eventually, much to Chandrakirti's delight, Avalokiteshvara appeared directly before him. Wishing to give the local people a chance to see Avalokiteshvara, Chandrakirti requested him to sit on the crown of his head while he walked around the town. Knowing that ordinary people did not have sufficiently pure minds to see a Buddha, Avalokiteshvara initially refused, but when Chandrakirti persisted in his requests Avalokiteshvara eventually accepted. Chandrakirti set off through the streets exhorting the people to make prostrations to the Buddha on his head. Most people saw nothing and assumed that Chandrakirti had gone mad, while a few people, with particularly heavy karmic obstructions, saw the corpse of a dog on his head! Only one person, an old woman wine-seller, saw the actual form of Avalokiteshvara, and she saw only his legs. Even so, this experience was so powerful that as a result she later achieved many profound realizations.

In a previous age a messenger once took shelter in a cave in which there was a wall-painting of Buddha Kashyapa.[20] Seeing the form of this Buddha, he developed great faith and yearned to see an actual Buddha. As a result, he later took a human rebirth as Shariputra, one of Buddha Shakyamuni's foremost disciples, and achieved liberation in that life.

A wild boar was once being chased through a forest by a hunter. Just as it was at the point of collapse, the terrified animal reached a clearing in which stood a stupa, a symbolic representation of Buddha's mind. Overcome by exhaustion, the boar collapsed and died. As a result of seeing the stupa, the boar's mind received Buddha's

Water Deity

blessings, and through the power of these blessings it was able to die peacefully and take rebirth in the god realm.

Hearing Buddha's speech, or a representation of his speech, or listening to or recalling the name of a Buddha, is just as beneficial. For example, there was once a pigeon that used to listen to Vasubhandu[21] while he recited the Sutras. As a result of the blessings the pigeon received from hearing the sound of the Sutras it subsequently took rebirth in the human realm as one of Vasubandhu's disciples and became a very famous scholar called Stirmati.

Through reciting the names of the Thirty-five Buddhas, many of Je Tsongkhapa's disciples received visions of them. The reason we do not see pure beings such as Buddhas and Bodhisattvas is that our minds are obstructed by negative karma and delusions, not because they are not there before us. For example, on an overcast day we cannot see the sun, but this does not mean that the sun does not exist. When we succeed in purifying the cloud-like delusions and negative karma that obscure our minds, we will be able to see Buddhas directly, and then we will find it easy to accomplish all the Mahayana realizations.

So as to increase our enthusiasm for purification practices and our faith and respect for the Buddhas, we should contemplate as follows:

All the problems I have experienced since beginningless time, and all the problems I will experience in the future, result from my negative karma. Therefore nothing can be more beneficial than to practise purification sincerely.

Buddhas are perfect witnesses to confession. Through the power of their blessings it is possible to purify all the negative karma I have accumulated since beginningless time. This opportunity to engage in purification is solely due to the kindness of the Buddhas.

God of Water Deities

The visualization

In the space in front of us we visualize Buddha Shakyamuni seated on a jewelled throne supported by eight white elephants, which symbolize the power of purification. He sits in the vajra posture on cushions of a lotus, a moon, and a sun. The lotus symbolizes renunciation, the moon symbolizes bodhichitta, and the sun symbolizes wisdom directly realizing emptiness.

Buddha wears the saffron robes of a fully ordained monk. Serene and majestic, his bearing is that of one who has passed beyond all worldly concerns. Gracing his crown is an ushnisha, demonstrating that he has always regarded his Spiritual Guide as supreme. His left hand rests in his lap in the gesture of meditative equipoise and holds a begging bowl filled with nectar, which reveals his transcendence of death, delusions, and the torment of an impure body and mind. The middle finger of his right hand touches the ground, calling the earth to witness his victory over the Devaputra demons.[22] Smiling gently, his clear eyes gaze at us with the love of a father for his dearest child. Fearless like the king of the lions, his radiance dispels the fears of all who behold him.

His golden body is made of light and is resplendent with the thirty-two signs and eighty indications of a fully enlightened being.[23] Like a universal sun, his brilliance pierces the shrouds of ignorance obscuring the minds of living beings. His deep and melodious voice reverberates throughout infinite worlds, ripening seeds of virtue and revealing liberating paths. His purified mind abides eternally in the tranquil ocean of reality, seeing all phenomena as clearly as a jewel held in the hand, and suffused with an all-embracing compassion. He is the ultimate refuge of all living beings.

In front of Buddha Shakyamuni are the remaining thirty-four Buddhas, seated in five rows. In the first row,

Glorious Excellence

closest to Buddha Shakyamuni, are the first six Buddhas: Complete Subduer with the Essence of Vajra, Jewel of Radiant Light, Powerful King of the Nagas, Leader of the Heroes, Glorious Pleasure, and Jewel Fire, arranged from left to right as we look at them. In front of these, and lower still, are the next seven Buddhas: Jewel Moonlight, Meaningful to Behold, Jewel Moon, Stainless One, Bestower of Glory, Pure One, and Transforming with Purity. In front of these, and slightly lower, are the seven Buddhas: Water Deity, God of Water Deities, Glorious Excellence, Glorious Sandalwood, Endless Splendour, Glorious Light, and Glorious One without Sorrow. In front of these are the seven Buddhas: Son without Craving, Glorious Flower, Clearly Knowing through Enjoying Pure Radiance, Clearly Knowing through Enjoying Lotus Radiance, Glorious Wealth, Glorious Mindfulness, and Glorious Name of Great Renown. Finally, in the row nearest to us are the remaining seven Buddhas: King of the Victory Banner Head of the Powerful Ones, Glorious One Complete Subduer, Great Victor in Battle, Glorious One Complete Subduer Passed Beyond, Glorious Array Illuminating All, Jewel Lotus Great Subduer, and King of Mount Meru. All these Buddhas sit on jewelled thrones on cushions of a lotus, a moon, and a sun. This assembly of Thirty-five Confession Buddhas is surrounded by all the Buddhas and Bodhisattvas of the ten directions.

We should regard each Buddha's body as the synthesis of all Sangha Jewels, each Buddha's speech as the synthesis of all Dharma Jewels, and each Buddha's mind as the synthesis of all Buddha Jewels. It does not matter if we cannot perceive the visualization clearly; the important thing is to generate deep faith and have no doubt that we are actually in the presence of real, living Buddhas.

We should know the name of each Buddha, the world over which he presides, his colour, his hand gestures, the

Glorious Sandalwood

objects that he holds, and the particular negative karma that is purified by reciting his name. The hand gestures and the objects held by each Buddha can be learned by studying the drawings in this book. The remaining features are listed in the chart on pages 57 – 59.

The actual practice

The actual practice of the *Sutra of Three Superior Heaps* is explained in three parts:

1 Purifying non-virtuous actions
2 Dedicating virtue
3 Conclusion

Purifying non-virtuous actions

Most of the non-virtuous actions we have committed since beginningless time are included within the ten non-virtuous actions: killing, stealing, sexual misconduct, lying, divisive speech, hurtful speech, idle gossip, covetousness, malice, and holding wrong views. These are explained in detail in *Joyful Path of Good Fortune.* We have to purify all these non-virtues together with all our downfalls of the Pratimoksha, Bodhisattva, and Tantric vows.

It is impossible to alter the fact that a negative action has been committed, but it is possible to eradicate the potential of a negative action to produce suffering. Every non-virtuous action has four potentials, each of which has its own effect: the ripening effect, the environmental effect, the effect that is an experience similar to the cause, and the effect that is a tendency similar to the cause. A detailed explanation of these four effects can be found in *Joyful Path of Good Fortune.* To purify these four potentials Buddha taught the four opponent powers, which are all contained within this Sutra.

Endless Splendour

NAME	WORLD	COLOUR	PURIFIES
Buddha Shakyamuni	Unforgetting World (this world)	Golden	All the negative actions accumulated over 10,000 aeons
Complete Subduer with the Essence of Vajra	Essence of Space (above this world)	Blue	All the negative actions accumulated over 10,000 aeons
Jewel of Radiant Light	Adorned with Jewels (east)	White	All the negative actions accumulated over 25,000 aeons
Powerful King of the Nagas	Pervaded by Nagas (south-east)	Blue	All the negative actions accumulated over eight aeons
Leader of the Heroes	Pervaded by Heroes (south)	Yellow	Negative karma of speech
Glorious Pleasure	Joyful (south-west)	Orange	Negative karma of mind
Jewel Fire	Pervaded by Light (west)	Red	Causing a schism within the Sangha
Jewel Moonlight	Excellent Light (north-west)	White	All the negative actions accumulated over one aeon
Meaningful to Behold	Sound of the Drum (north)	Green	Criticizing Superior beings [24]
Jewel Moon	Adorned with Light-rays (north-east)	White	Killing one's mother
Stainless One	Pervaded by Dust (below this world)	Smoke-coloured	Killing one's father
Bestower of Glory	The Glorious (above this world)	White	Killing a Foe Destroyer [25]

57

NAME	WORLD	COLOUR	PURIFIES
Pure One	Unobstructed (east)	Orange	Maliciously wounding a Buddha
Transforming with Purity	Sorrowless (south-east)	Yellow	All the negative actions accumulated over 10,000 aeons
Water Deity	Stainless (south)	Blue	Raping nuns or Foe Destroyers
God of Water Deities	Perfectly Clear (south-west)	White	Killing Bodhisattvas
Glorious Excellence	Blissful (west)	Red	Killing Learner Superiors [26]
Glorious Sandalwood	Pervaded by Fragrance (north-west)	Orange	Stealing from the Sangha
Endless Splendour	Possessing Vitality (north)	Red	Destroying stupas
Glorious Light	Meaningful (north-east)	White	Negative actions committed out of hatred
Glorious One without Sorrow	Unobstructed (below)	Pale blue	Negative actions committed out of attachment
Son without Craving	Free from Attachment (above)	Blue	All the negative actions accumulated over 10,000 aeons
Glorious Flower	Increasing Flowers (east)	Yellow	All the negative actions accumulated over 100,000 aeons
Clearly Knowing through Enjoying Pure Radiance	Pervaded by Brahmas (south-east)	White	All the negative actions accumulated over 1,000 aeons

NAME	WORLD	COLOUR	PURIFIES
Clearly Knowing through Enjoying Lotus Radiance	Adorned with Lotuses (south)	Red	All the negative actions accumulated over seven aeons
Glorious Wealth	Adorned with Jewels (south-west)	Pink	Negativity arising from bad habits
Glorious Mindfulness	Perfectly Clear (west)	Yellow	Negative karma of body
Glorious Name of Great Renown	Signless (north-west)	Green	Displeasing Buddhas
King of the Victory Banner	Clear Sense Power (north)	Yellow	Negative actions committed out of jealousy
Glorious One Complete Subduer	Enjoyment (north-east)	White	Commanding others to commit negative actions
Great Victor in Battle	Without delusion (below)	Black	Negative actions committed out of pride
Glorious One Complete Subduer Passed Beyond	The Glorious (east)	White	Slander
Glorious Array Illuminating All	Adorned with Light (south)	Yellow	Rejoicing in evil
Jewel Lotus Great Subduer	The Glorious (west)	Red	Abandoning Dharma
King of Mount Meru	Jewel (north)	Clear blue	Breaking commitments

Glorious Light

The first opponent power, the power of reliance, purifies the potential for the environmental effect and also functions to subdue negative karma in general. The second opponent power, the power of the antidote, purifies the potential for the ripening effect and also acts as the direct antidote to negative karma in general. The third opponent power, the power of regret, purifies the potential for the effect that is an experience similar to the cause and functions to prevent the power of negative karma from increasing. The fourth opponent power, the power of promise, purifies the potential for the effect that is a tendency similar to the cause and prevents us from repeating the action. The degree to which we succeed in purifying negative karma depends upon our skill in applying these four opponent powers.

From this we can understand that sincerely taking refuge in the Three Jewels, even without an intention to purify, functions to subdue our negative karma and to weaken the potential to experience an unpleasant environmental effect. For example, we may be born in hell as a consequence of not having purified the ripening effect of a severely negative action, but the duration of our stay there will be shortened if we have previously taken refuge. Similarly, if we commit a negative action and then immediately generate regret, although regret by itself does not have the power to purify the action completely, it will prevent the power of the action increasing and also weaken its potential to produce an experience similar to the cause.

The way to apply the four opponent powers within the practice of the *Sutra of the Three Superior Heaps* will now be explained under the following four headings:

1 The power of reliance
2 The power of the antidote
3 The power of regret
4 The power of promise

Glorious One without Sorrow

THE POWER OF RELIANCE

Focusing our mind on the visualized assembly of Thirty-five Buddhas, and recognizing them as the essence of all Buddha Jewels, Dharma Jewels, and Sangha Jewels, we generate deep faith and go for refuge while reciting the following lines from the Sutra:

I, whose name is . . . , at all times go for refuge to the Guru, go for refuge to the Buddha, go for refuge to the Dharma, go for refuge to the Sangha.

While we are reciting this, we should mentally generate bodhichitta, thinking: 'I must attain Buddhahood for the sake of all mother sentient beings.'

THE POWER OF THE ANTIDOTE

With the strong faith and conviction we developed by going for refuge, we now make physical prostrations while reciting the name of each Buddha as a request for them to purify our negative karma. There are three ways to make physical prostrations: making full-length prostrations by prostrating our whole body on the ground, making half-length prostrations by kneeling respectfully and touching our palms and our forehead to the ground, or making a gesture of respect such as pressing our palms together at our heart.

Prostrations are a powerful method for purifying negative karma, disease, and obstacles, and they increase our merit, our happiness, and our Dharma realizations. Temporarily prostrations improve our physical health and ultimately they cause us to obtain a Buddha's Form Body. A more extensive explanation of the benefits of prostrations can be found in *Joyful Path of Good Fortune*.

When we make prostrations to the Thirty-five Confession Buddhas we can either make one prostration to each Buddha as we recite his name, and then repeat the cycle as many times as we wish, or we can make a number of prostrations,

Son without Craving

say seven, twenty-one, fifty, or a hundred, to the first Buddha while reciting his name, and then go on to make the same number of prostrations to the second Buddha, and so on. If we do this we will probably not be able to complete the prostrations to all the Thirty-five Buddhas in one session, in which case we simply begin the next session where we left off.

Each Buddha's name has great meaning. There is not the space here to explain the meaning of all the names, but it may be helpful to understand the meaning of Buddha Shakyamuni's name. The Tibetan for 'Tathagata' is 'deshin shegpa', in which 'deshin' means ultimate truth, or emptiness, and 'shegpa' means gone. Thus, 'deshin shegpa' is a mind that has gone into, or completely mixed with, emptiness; in other words, it is the Wisdom Truth Body. Therefore, 'Tathagata' means that Buddha has achieved the Wisdom Truth Body and the Nature Body.[27] 'Foe Destroyer' indicates that Buddha has completely destroyed the obstructions to liberation.[28] 'Completely Perfect Buddha' affirms that he has attained great enlightenment and also indicates that he has attained the clear light of bliss and the illusory body.[29] He is called 'Glorious' because he is the Protector of living beings, and 'Conqueror' because he is victorious over the four maras. 'Muni' means 'Able One' and indicates that Buddha has the ability to free all sentient beings from the ocean of samsara. Since Buddha was born to the Shakya clan, he is called 'Shakyamuni'. All these titles, except 'Shakya', apply equally to all Buddhas. By contemplating these names, we come to understand the good qualities of the Buddhas and thereby strengthen our faith.

THE POWER OF REGRET

After reciting the names of the Buddhas together with making prostrations, we can either continue to prostrate

Glorious Flower

or sit down while we recite the rest of the Sutra. We recall that the Thirty-five Buddhas are in the space in front of us surrounded by all the Buddhas and Bodhisattvas of the ten directions. By reciting the following words from the Sutra we ask them to give us their attention and witness our confession:

O all you [Tathagatas] and all the others, however many Tathagatas, the Foe Destroyers, the Completely Perfect Buddhas, the Blessed Ones there are dwelling and abiding in all the worldly realms of the ten directions, all you Buddhas, the Blessed Ones, please listen to me.

We now acknowledge that in the past we have committed many heavy negative actions and, with great remorse, confess them as follows:

In this life and in all my lives since beginningless time, in all my places of rebirth whilst wandering in cyclic existence, I have done negative actions, have ordered them to be done, and have rejoiced in their being done. I have stolen the property of the bases of offering, the property of the Sangha, and the property of the Sanghas of the ten directions, have ordered it to be stolen, and have rejoiced in it being stolen. I have committed the five unbounded heinous actions, have ordered them to be committed, and have rejoiced in their being committed. I have completely engaged in the paths of the ten non-virtuous actions, have ordered others to engage in them, and have rejoiced in their engaging in them.

Here, the 'property of the bases of offering' is anything that has been offered to the Three Jewels. It includes offerings and donations for pujas;[30] for the construction of temples or other buildings used by Dharma communities; for statues, paintings, or stupas; or for the

Clearly Knowing through Enjoying Pure Radiance

publication of Dharma books – in short, anything that has been offered to or that belongs to a Dharma community. Stealing from a Dharma centre is extremely heavy negative karma that causes rebirth in hell or one of the other unfree states.[31] The 'property of the Sangha' is the belongings of individual Dharma practitioners, and the 'property of the Sanghas of the ten directions' is anything that belongs to the ordained Sangha community. The 'five unbounded heinous actions', otherwise known as the five actions of immediate retribution, are killing one's father, killing one's mother, killing a Foe Destroyer, maliciously wounding a Buddha, and causing a schism within the Sangha. Harming our Spiritual Guide is equivalent to the fourth, and deliberately causing a division within a Dharma community is equivalent to the fifth. We have committed actions such as these many times in previous lives and may even have done them in this life. Acknowledging this, we should try to generate strong regret by contemplating the fate that awaits us if we fail to purify these actions. We recite the following lines from the Sutra:

Being obstructed by such karmic obstructions, I shall become a hell being, or I shall be born as an animal, or I shall go to the land of the hungry ghosts, or I shall be born as a barbarian in an irreligious country, or I shall be born as a long-life god, or I shall come to have incomplete senses, or I shall come to hold wrong views, or I shall have no opportunity to please a Buddha.

These lines remind us that an effect of negative karma is rebirth in one of the eight unfree states. The meaning of the last line is that we will have no opportunity to meet, or to please, a Spiritual Guide.

Having acknowledged the extent of our negative karma, we now practise a special method for purifying it. At our heart, we visualize all the potentials of our

Clearly Knowing through Enjoying Lotus Radiance

negative actions in the form of a black letter PAM. We then imagine that the negative karma of all other sentient beings gathers in the aspect of smoke and dissolves into the PAM, and we think that the PAM has become the essence of all our own and others' negativity. We pray:

All such karmic obstructions I declare in the presence of the Buddhas, the Blessed Ones, who have become exalted wisdom, who have become 'eyes', who have become witnesses, who have become valid, who see with their wisdom. I confess without concealing or hiding anything, . . .

Then we imagine that white wisdom lights and nectars descend from the hearts of all the Thirty-five Buddhas and enter our body through the crown. When they reach the PAM they completely destroy it, just as a lamp destroys darkness as soon as it is switched on. We firmly believe that all our negative karma created since beginningless time has been purified. The wisdom lights pervade our body and mind increasing our lifespan, our good fortune, our physical and mental power, and our Dharma realizations.

Buddhas 'have become exalted wisdom' because they know the entire past, present, and future directly; and they 'have become eyes' because they watch all sentient beings with eyes of great compassion. Since Buddhas know everything and in particular because they are aware of the good and bad actions we have done in this and previous lives, they 'have become witnesses'. They 'have become valid' because they are non-deceptive objects of refuge, and they 'see with their wisdom' all the negative karma that we have committed in the past, as well as the suffering that will result from it.

THE POWER OF PROMISE

Unless we refrain from negative actions in the future it will be impossible to fully purify those we have already

Glorious Wealth

committed. If we think that it does not matter if we continue to commit negative actions because we have a method for purifying them, this shows that we do not understand purification. In the *Lion's Roar Sutra* Buddha says that he has taught the Dharma of the *Three Superior Heaps* to enable us to purify negative karma, but those who continue to perform negative actions thinking that they can purify them later are foolish. Therefore we must refrain from non-virtuous actions by making the following promise to the Buddhas:

> **. . . and from now on I shall avoid and refrain from such actions.**

Some practitioners can promise to refrain from every downfall and negative action for the rest of their lives and, by relying on mindfulness, conscientiousness, and alertness, never break this promise. If we are not yet able to make such a promise, we should first promise to refrain from all negative actions for one week, and then gradually extend the duration of our restraint to a month, a year, and so on, until we can promise to refrain for the rest of our life. It is important to keep whatever promises we have made to the Buddhas and to our Spiritual Guide because broken promises are serious obstacles to our spiritual progress.

Dedicating virtue

Generally, dedication ensures that virtuous actions produce great results. Here, we dedicate so that our purification practice will definitely produce great and powerful results in the future. We begin by requesting the Buddhas to witness our dedication:

> **All you Buddhas, the Blessed Ones, please listen to me.**

Then we review the virtuous actions to be dedicated:

Glorious Mindfulness

In this life and in all my previous lives since beginningless time, in all my places of rebirth whilst wandering in cyclic existence, whatever root of virtue there is in my giving to others, even in my giving a morsel of food to one born as an animal; whatever root of virtue there is in my maintaining moral discipline; whatever root of virtue there is in my actions conducive to great liberation; whatever root of virtue there is in my acting to fully ripen sentient beings; whatever root of virtue there is in my generating a supreme mind of enlightenment; and whatever root of virtue there is in my unsurpassed exalted wisdom; all of these assembled, gathered, and collected together, . . .

The first two types of virtue mentioned here, giving and moral discipline, are self-explanatory. The third, 'actions conducive to great liberation', refers to the remaining four perfections – patience, effort, mental stabilization, and wisdom – which are the means to achieve the great liberation of Buddhahood. 'Acting to fully ripen sentient beings' refers to the four ways of gathering disciples.[32] Whereas the virtues listed previously principally function to ripen our own mental continuum, the four ways of gathering disciples principally function to ripen others' mental continuums. 'Generating a supreme mind of enlightenment' refers to the generation of bodhichitta and 'unsurpassed exalted wisdom' refers to any spiritual realization of a person on an actual Hinayana or Mahayana path. If we have not yet developed spontaneous renunciation or bodhichitta we do not possess such exalted wisdom, but we can appreciate the exalted wisdom of others and dedicate their virtues. 'All of these assembled' means the collection of all our own virtues produced by these actions, 'gathered' refers to the collection of all other beings' virtues, and 'collected together' refers to

Glorious Name of Great Renown

our own and others' virtues united together. All of this is what is to be dedicated. As for the purpose for which it is dedicated, the Sutra continues:

. . . by fully dedicating them to the unsurpassed, to that of which there is no higher, to that which is even higher than the high, and to that which surpasses the unsurpassed, I fully dedicate to the unsurpassed, perfect, complete enlightenment.

Just as the Buddhas, the Blessed Ones of the past, have dedicated fully, just as the Buddhas, the Blessed Ones who are yet to come, will dedicate fully, and just as the Buddhas, the Blessed Ones who are living now, dedicate fully, so too do I dedicate fully.

The 'unsurpassed' refers to a Buddha's Form Body, which arises from unsurpassed merit; 'that of which there is no higher' refers to a Buddha's Truth Body, which arises from the highest wisdom; 'even higher than the high' refers to a Buddha's Emanation Bodies, which are even higher than Hinayana Foe Destroyers to whom they give teachings; and 'that which surpasses the unsurpassed' refers to a Buddha's Enjoyment Body, which surpasses Superior Bodhisattvas, who themselves are unsurpassed by any other sentient being. In short, by reciting this dedication prayer we dedicate all the virtues of ourselves and others to the attainment of a Buddha's Form Body and a Buddha's Truth Body so that we shall be able to benefit all sentient beings.

The benefits of this dedication can be understood by considering the effects of a simple action such as giving. If we do not make any dedication at all it is probable that the potential to produce happiness created by our virtuous action of giving will soon be destroyed by anger or wrong views. This danger can be avoided by dedicating the virtue for some mundane purpose. If we do this, we will experience a beneficial effect such as wealth in the future, but as soon as this is used up the positive potential of our original action will also have been exhausted. However, if we make the supreme dedication as mentioned in this Sutra, the potential power of that simple act of giving will never be exhausted, no matter how much we enjoy its temporary fruits. For example, if a drop of water is taken from a spring and put into an ocean it will not evaporate until the ocean itself dries up. In a similar fashion, if we dedicate our virtue of giving to full enlightenment, it will not be exhausted until enlightenment is attained. Therefore its results are infinite. The same applies to all other virtues. All the Buddhas of the past dedicated in this way while they were Bodhisattvas, and now they are experiencing the beneficial results of their dedication. We should follow their example and dedicate in the same way.

Conclusion

We continue the recitation of the Sutra with a brief prayer:

I confess individually all negative actions. I rejoice in all merit. I beseech and request all the Buddhas. May I attain the holy, supreme, unsurpassed, exalted wisdom.

Confession purifies negative karma in general, rejoicing purifies negativities caused by jealousy, beseeching Buddhas not to pass away purifies actions that disturb our Spiritual Guide, and requesting them to turn the Wheel of Dharma purifies the negative action of abandoning Dharma. The virtues of this short prayer are dedicated to the attainment of the supreme, unsurpassed, exalted wisdom, in other words Buddha's omniscient wisdom.

The last lines of the Sutra explicitly teach refuge in the Buddhas of the three times and implicitly reveal refuge in Dharma and Sangha:

Whoever are the Conquerors, the supreme beings living now, those of the past, and likewise those who are yet to come, with a boundless ocean of praise for all your good qualities, and with my palms pressed together I go close to you for refuge.

The essential meaning of these lines is that the practice of the three superior heaps – prostration, purification, and dedication – should be combined with refuge in the Three Jewels.

The best way to avoid committing negative actions or downfalls is always to maintain a good heart through the practice of the twenty-one meditations explained in *A Meditation Handbook*, and the best method for purifying negative actions and downfalls already accumulated is to practise the *Sutra of the Three Superior Heaps*. With these two practices we shall be able to safeguard the whole of our Bodhisattva's way of life.

King of the Victory Banner

Training in the Six Perfections

THE ACTUAL TRAININGS OF A BODHISATTVA

Maintaining the Bodhisattva vows is the basis for the actual trainings of the Bodhisattva. These are all included within the practice of the six perfections: the perfection of giving, the perfection of moral discipline, the perfection of patience, the perfection of effort, the perfection of mental stabilization, and the perfection of wisdom. If we wish to become enlightened but do not engage in these actions we are like someone who wants to go to India but does not actually make the journey.

The perfection of giving

Giving is defined as a virtuous mental decision to give, or a physical or verbal action of giving that is motivated by a virtuous state of mind. Giving that is motivated by bodhichitta is a perfection of giving. There are three kinds of giving:

1 Giving material things
2 Giving Dharma
3 Giving fearlessness

Giving material things

To practise giving material things, we first contemplate the disadvantages of miserliness and the benefits of giving and then we engage in the actual practice of giving to others. Buddha taught that miserliness leads to poverty and rebirth as a hungry spirit. Even in this life miserliness causes us suffering. It is a tight, uncomfortable mind that leads to isolation and unpopularity. Giving, on the other hand, is a joyful mind that leads us to experience wealth and abundant resources in the future.

There is no point in clinging to our possessions, for wealth acquires meaning only when it is given away or used to benefit others. Since, without any choice, we shall have to part with all our possessions when we die, it is better to part with them now and derive some benefit from having owned them. Moreover, if at the time of our death we have strong attachment to our possessions this will prevent us from having a peaceful death and may even prevent us from taking a fortunate rebirth.

When we go on holiday we take care to carry enough money to see us through the whole holiday, but how much more important it is to ensure that we travel to future lives with enough virtue to provide us with all the resources we shall need. Our practice of giving is the best insurance against future poverty.

We should give away our possessions only when the time is right, that is, when it would not cause any hindrances to our spiritual practice or endanger our life, and when the person to whom we are giving will derive great benefit. Otherwise, we should not give away our possessions even if someone asks for them. For example, if we can see that a gift will cause harm to others we should not offer it. We need to consider all the implications of our action, including how it will affect others besides the person who is to receive the gift. We also need to keep those things that are necessary for our Dharma practice. If we were to give these away we would be indirectly harming others because we would be creating obstacles to our progress towards enlightenment for their sake.

We should mentally dedicate all our possessions to others but we should physically give them away only when it is most suitable to do so. This skilful way of thinking is in itself a form of giving. For example, charitable organisations do not immediately give away everything that is donated to them, but keep a certain amount in reserve for when it is most needed. Even so, while they are holding on to the money they do not consider it to be their own; they simply think that they are looking after it for others until a need arises. If we view all our possessions in a similar way we shall be practising giving all the time.

The amount of merit we accumulate by the practice of giving depends upon several factors besides the actual value of the gift. One factor is the nature of the recipient. There are three classes of being to whom it is especially meritorious to give: holy beings, such as our Spiritual Guide, Buddhas, and Bodhisattvas; those who have shown us great kindness, such as our parents; and beings who are in great need, such as the poor, the sick, and the handicapped. Another important factor is our motivation. It is more meritorious to put a few crumbs on a bird table with a motivation of pure compassion than it is to give a diamond ring out of attachment. The best motivation, of course, is bodhichitta. The virtue created by giving with this motivation is limitless.

Giving Dharma

There are many ways to give Dharma. If, with a good motivation, we teach even just one word of Dharma to others, we are giving Dharma. This is much more beneficial than any kind of material gift because material things help others in this life alone whereas the gift of Dharma helps them in this and all their future lives. There are many other ways in which we can give Dharma, for

Glorious One Complete Subduer

example, by dedicating our virtue so that all beings may enjoy peace and happiness, or by whispering mantras into the ears of animals.

Giving fearlessness

To give fearlessness is to protect other beings from fear or danger. For example, if we rescue someone from a fire or from some other natural disaster, if we protect others from physical violence, or if we save animals who have fallen into water or who are trapped, we are practising giving fearlessness. If we are not able to rescue those in danger, we can still give fearlessness by making prayers and offerings so that others may be released from danger. We can also practise giving fearlessness by praying for others to become free from their delusions, especially the delusion of self-grasping, which is the ultimate source of all fear.

The perfection of moral discipline

Moral discipline is a virtuous mental determination to abandon any fault, or it is a physical or verbal action motivated by such a determination. Moral discipline practised with bodhichitta motivation is a perfection of moral discipline. There are three kinds of moral discipline:

1 The moral discipline of restraint
2 The moral discipline of gathering virtuous Dharmas
3 The moral discipline of benefiting living beings

The moral discipline of restraint

This is the moral discipline of abstaining from non-virtue. To practise this moral discipline we need to understand the dangers of committing negative actions and then make and keep a vow or a promise to abandon them. Simply failing to commit negative actions unintentionally is not a practice of moral discipline because it is not motivated by a determination to abstain.

Any spiritual discipline that avoids or overcomes either mental faults or negative actions of body or speech is included within the moral discipline of restraint. For example, if we understand the dangers of the ten non-virtuous actions and we promise to refrain from them and keep that promise, we are practising the moral discipline of restraint.

Sometimes we can take vows by ourselves by recognizing the faults of the actions we want to abandon and promising to refrain from them for whatever length of time we can. Even if we promise to abstain from just one negative action for only a short time, for example if we promise only to abandon killing for just one week, and we keep that promise, we are practising the moral discipline of restraint. However, as our capacity increases we should gradually extend the duration of our restraint, and also promise to abandon other non-virtuous actions as well.

To practise moral discipline we need to rely on mindfulness, alertness, and conscientiousness. Mindfulness prevents us from forgetting our vows, alertness keeps a check on our mind and warns us if delusions are about to arise, and conscientiousness protects our mind from non-virtue. For example, we may be in a situation, such as a lively party, in which it would be easy to incur the downfall of praising ourself and scorning others. However, if we practise mindfulness we will constantly remember that we have promised not to do such things and there will be no danger of our incurring this downfall out of forgetfulness. Similarly, if we maintain alertness we will be able to detect delusions such as pride or envy as soon as they begin to arise and then use conscientiousness to check their development.

When we take the Bodhisattva vows we must have the intention to keep them continuously until we are enlightened.

If we are to fulfil our wish to attain enlightenment quickly for the sake of others, we need to overcome our faults as soon as we can. For a Bodhisattva, the main object to be abandoned is the intention to work solely for one's own sake. Bodhisattvas see clearly the dangers of self-cherishing and they realize that it is the principal obstacle to developing bodhichitta and to achieving enlightenment. In the *Condensed Perfection of Wisdom Sutra* Buddha says that the moral discipline of a Bodhisattva does not degenerate if he enjoys beautiful forms, sounds, tastes, or other objects of the senses, but if a Bodhisattva develops concern for his own welfare both his moral discipline and his bodhichitta degenerate. If we generate bodhichitta and later think that it would be better to seek only our own liberation we incur a root Bodhisattva downfall and break our moral discipline of restraint.

With the motivation of bodhichitta, no action can be non-virtuous because bodhichitta eliminates self-cherishing which is the root of all non-virtuous actions. Even if a Bodhisattva has to kill, this action is not non-virtuous because it is performed solely for the benefit of all living beings. Although others may condemn them, Bodhisattvas receive no bad karma when they perform such actions because their bodhichitta ensures that all their actions are pure. This is illustrated by an episode from a previous life of Buddha Shakyamuni while he was still a Bodhisattva. At that time he was the captain of a ship that was ferrying five hundred merchants across the sea. With his clairvoyance he saw that one of the merchants was planning to kill all the others. Seeing that as a result of this that merchant would be reborn in hell, he generated great compassion for him and for his intended victims. He decided to take upon himself the karma of killing rather than allow all five hundred merchants to suffer and so, with pure bodhichitta motivation, he killed the wicked merchant. In this way he protected that merchant

Great Victor in Battle

from a hellish rebirth and saved the lives of all the others. As a result of this action of killing, the Bodhisattva made great spiritual progress.

The moral discipline of gathering virtuous Dharmas

We practise this moral discipline when we sincerely practise any virtuous action such as keeping the Bodhisattva vows purely, practising the six perfections, making offerings to the Three Jewels, or putting energy into studying, meditating on, or propagating the holy Dharma.

The moral discipline of benefiting living beings

This is the moral discipline of helping others in whatever way we can. If we cannot offer practical help to someone, we can at least make prayers for them and maintain a continuous intention to give assistance when an opportunity arises. We can understand how to practise this moral discipline by studying the instructions on the last eleven secondary downfalls of the Bodhisattva vows.

When we help others, we should be tactful and sensitive. We should try to understand the other person's experience and point of view and then offer help that is relevant to them, and in such a way that they can accept it. We cannot help others if we attack their values and beliefs, or if we completely ignore their temperament and their personal circumstances. We have to adapt our own behaviour so that it suits the other person and makes them feel at ease. Instead of imposing our moral standards on others and passing judgement on them if they do not comply, we should simply act in the way that will have the most positive effect. We need both flexibility of mind and flexibility of behaviour.

Since Bodhisattvas have great compassion they do whatever is necessary to help others. In effect, Bodhisattvas will do whatever needs to be done to make someone else happy because when others are happy their minds are more open and receptive to advice and example. If we wish to influence others we can do so only if we do not antagonize them or make them feel uncomfortable or frightened.

The tact and sensitivity required by a Bodhisattva when helping others is well illustrated by an episode from the life of Geshe Langri Tangpa.[33] A woman who had recently given birth to a baby girl was frightened she would lose her baby because she had already given birth to one child who had died while it was still an infant. The woman expressed her anxiety to her mother who told her that children given into the care of Geshe Langri Tangpa would not die. Later, when the little girl fell ill, the woman took her to see Geshe Langri Tangpa, but when she arrived, she found him sitting on a throne giving a discourse to a thousand disciples. The woman began to worry that the child would die before the end of the discourse. She knew that Geshe Langri Tangpa was a Bodhisattva and would show patience, and so she walked up to the throne and, in a loud, affronted tone of voice, declared, 'Here, take your baby. Now you look after her!' She turned to the audience and said, 'This is the father of my child', and then turned back to Geshe Langri Tangpa and pleaded softly, 'Please don't let her die.' Geshe Langri Tangpa just nodded his head in acceptance. As if he really were the father of the child, he wrapped it tenderly in his robes and continued his discourse. His disciples were astounded and asked him, 'Are you really the father of that child?' Knowing that if he were to deny it, the woman would have been thought crazy and the people would have ridiculed her, Geshe Langri Tangpa replied that he was.

Although he was a monk, Geshe Langri Tangpa acted like a real father for the child, delighting in her and caring for her. After some time, the mother returned to see if her daughter was well. When she saw how healthy the child was she asked Geshe Langri Tangpa if she could have her back again. The Geshe then kindly returned the girl to her mother. When his disciples realized what had happened they said, 'So you are not really the father after all!' and Geshe Langri Tangpa said, 'No, I am not.' In this way, Geshe Langri Tangpa responded to the woman's actions with pure compassion and acted in accordance with the needs of the time.

The perfection of patience

Patience is a virtuous mind that is able to bear harm, suffering, or profound Dharma. Patience practised with bodhichitta motivation is a perfection of patience.

Even if we have no interest in spiritual development patience is an important quality to cultivate because without it we remain vulnerable to anxiety, frustration, and disquiet. If we lack patience it is difficult to maintain peaceful relationships with others.

Patience is the antidote to anger, the most potent destroyer of virtue. We can see from our own experience how much suffering arises from anger. It prevents us from judging a situation correctly and causes us to act in regrettable ways. It destroys our own peace of mind and disturbs everyone else we meet. Even people who are normally attracted to us are repelled when they see us angry. Anger can make us reject or abuse our own parents. When it is intense, it can even drive us to kill the people we love, or even to take our own life.

Usually anger is triggered by something quite insignificant, such as a comment that we take personally, a habit that we find irritating, or an expectation that was not fulfilled. Based on such small experiences, anger

Glorious One Complete Subduer Passed Beyond

weaves an elaborate fantasy, exaggerating the unpleasantness of the situation, and providing rationalizations and justifications for the sense of outrage or resentment. It leads us to say and do harmful things, thereby causing offence to others and transforming a small difficulty into a great problem.

If we were asked 'Who caused all the wars in which so many people have died?', we would have to reply that they were caused by angry minds. If nations were full of calm, peace-loving people, how could wars ever arise? Anger is the greatest enemy of living beings. It harmed us in the past, it harms us now, and, if we do not overcome it through the practice of patience, it will continue to harm us in the future. As Shantideva says:

This enemy of anger has no function
Other than to cause me harm.

External enemies harm us in slower and less subtle ways, and if we practise patience with them we can even win them over and turn them into our friends, but there can be no reconciliation with anger. If we are lenient with anger it will take advantage of us and harm us even more. Moreover, whereas external enemies can harm us only in this life, anger harms us for many future lives. Therefore, we need to eliminate anger as soon as it enters our mind because if we do not it will quickly become a blazing fire that consumes our merit.

Patience, on the other hand, helps us in this life and in all future lives. Shantideva says:

There is no evil like anger
And no virtue like patience.

With patience, we can accept any pain that is inflicted upon us and we can easily endure our usual troubles and indispositions. With patience, nothing upsets our peace of mind and we do not experience problems. With patience, we maintain an inner peace and tranquility that allows spiritual realizations to grow. Chandrakirti says that if we practise patience we will have a beautiful form in the future, and we will become a holy being with high realizations.

There are three kinds of patience:

1 The patience of not retaliating
2 The patience of voluntarily enduring suffering
3 The patience of definitely thinking about Dharma

The patience of not retaliating

To practise this type of patience we need to remain continuously mindful of the dangers of anger and the benefits of patient acceptance, and whenever anger is about to arise we need immediately to apply the methods for eliminating it. We have to begin by learning to forbear small difficulties such as insignificant abuse or minor disruptions in our routine, and then gradually improve our patience until we are able to forbear even the greatest difficulty without getting angry.

When we are meditating on patience we can use many different lines of reasoning to help us overcome our tendency to retaliate. For example, we can contemplate that if someone were to hit us with a stick we would not get angry with the stick because it was being wielded by the attacker and had no choice. In the same way, if someone abuses us or harms us, we should not get angry with them because they are being manipulated by their deluded minds and also have no choice. Similarly, we can think that, just as a doctor does not get angry if a feverish patient lashes out at him, so we should not get angry if confused sentient beings suffering from the sickness of the delusions harm us in any way. There are many special lines of reasoning such as these to be found in *Joyful Path of Good Fortune* and *Meaningful to Behold*.

The fundamental reason why we receive harm is that we have harmed others in the past. Those who attack us are merely the conditions whereby our karma ripens; the real cause of all the harm we receive is our own negativity. If in such circumstances we retaliate, we simply create more negative karma and so we will have to suffer even more harm in the future. By patiently accepting injury, however, the chain is broken and that particular karmic debt is paid off.

The patience of voluntarily enduring suffering

If we do not have the patience of voluntarily enduring suffering we become discouraged whenever we encounter obstacles and whenever our wishes go unfulfilled. We find it hard to complete our tasks because we feel like abandoning them as soon as they become difficult, and our miseries are further aggravated by our impatience. However, it is possible to accept and endure pain if we have a good reason to do so, and whenever we practise such patience we actually reduce our sufferings. For example, if someone were to stick a sharp needle into our flesh we would find the pain unbearable, but if the needle contained a vaccine that we needed, our tolerance would increase considerably.

Even to succeed in worldly aims people are prepared to endure adversity. Businessmen sacrifice their leisure and peace of mind just to make money, and soldiers put up with extreme hardship simply to kill other soldiers. How much more willing should we be to bear difficulties for the sake of the most worthwhile aim of all – the attainment of enlightenment for the benefit of all living beings.

Because we are in samsara we often have to endure unpleasant conditions and misfortune. With the patience of voluntarily enduring suffering, however, we can

Glorious Array Illuminating All

happily and courageously accept these adversities whenever they arise. When our wishes are not fulfilled, or when we are sick, bereaved, or otherwise in difficulty, we should not be discouraged. Instead of feeling self-pity, we should use our suffering to strengthen our spiritual practice. We can recall that all our suffering is the result of our previous negative karma and resolve to practise pure moral discipline in the future; or we can contemplate that for as long as we remain in samsara suffering is inevitable and thereby increase our renunciation; or we can use our own suffering as an illustration of the much greater suffering experienced by other beings and in this way strengthen our compassion.

If we are able to endure adversities we will reap great rewards. Our present sufferings will diminish and we will accomplish both our temporary and our ultimate wishes. Thus, suffering should not be seen as an obstacle to our spiritual practice but as an indispensable aid. As Shantideva says:

> Moreover, suffering has good qualities.
> Because of sorrow, pride is dispelled,
> Compassion arises for those trapped in cyclic existence,
> Evil is shunned, and joy is found in virtue.

The patience of definitely thinking about Dharma

If we listen to, contemplate, or meditate on Dharma with a patient and joyful mind so as to gain a special experience of Dharma, we are practising the patience of definitely thinking about Dharma. Such patience is important because if our mind is impatient or unhappy when we engage in Dharma practice this will obstruct our spiritual progress and prevent us from improving our Dharma wisdom. Even if we find some aspects of our Dharma practice difficult, we still need to engage in them with a happy mind.

The perfection of effort

Effort is a mind that delights in virtue. Effort practised with bodhichitta motivation is a perfection of effort. Applying ourselves energetically to non-virtuous or neutral actions, however, is not a practice of effort.

Effort is not something to be practised separately, but a practice that should accompany all our virtuous endeavours. We practise effort when we apply ourselves enthusiastically to Dharma study or meditation, strive to accomplish Dharma realizations, or put effort into helping others.

With effort we can achieve mundane and supramundane happiness.[34] It enables us to complete those virtuous actions that cause birth in the fortunate realms as well as those that lead to liberation and enlightenment. We can purify all our negativities and achieve whatever good qualities we wish for. Without effort, even if our wisdom is sharp, we shall be unable to complete our spiritual practices.

To generate effort we need to overcome the three types of laziness: procrastination, attraction to what is meaningless or non-virtuous, and discouragement. Procrastination is a reluctance or unwillingness to put effort into spiritual practice immediately. For example, although we may have an interest in Dharma and intend to practise it, we may feel that we can postpone our practice until some point in the future – when we have had a holiday, when the children have grown up, or when we retire. This is a dangerous attitude because the opportunity to practise Dharma is so easily lost. Death can strike at any time. Moreover, when we have finished the particular task that is presently preventing us from practising Dharma, we can be certain that another will arise to take its place. Worldly activities are like an old man's beard – though he may shave it off in the morning, it has grown again by the evening. Therefore, we should abandon procrastination and begin to practise Dharma immediately. The best remedy for the laziness of procrastination is to meditate on our precious human rebirth and on death and impermanence.[35]

Most of us are very familiar with the second type of laziness. We give into it whenever we watch television for hours on end without caring what comes on, or when we indulge in prolonged conversations with no purpose, or when we become engrossed in sports or business ventures for their own sake. Activities such as these dissipate the energy we have for practising Dharma. Though they may seem pleasant they deceive us, wasting our precious human life and destroying our opportunity to achieve real and lasting happiness. To overcome this type of laziness we need to meditate again and again on the dangers of cyclic existence, remembering that all the entertainments of worldly life are deceptive because, in reality, they serve only to bind us within samsara and cause us even more suffering.

The laziness of discouragement is very common in these degenerate times. Since we cannot see with our own eyes living examples of enlightened beings, and since our spiritual progress is often much slower than we expect it to be, we may begin to doubt whether Buddhahood is possible, or we may conclude that it must be so rare that there is almost no hope of attaining it. We may also see faults in our Spiritual Guide and in those who are practising Dharma and conclude that they have no realizations and that effort put into Dharma practice is wasted. If we find we are becoming discouraged in this way we need to remember that every appearance to the minds of ordinary beings is mistaken because it is contaminated by ignorance. However, we can be certain that when through practising Dharma sincerely we eliminate our ignorance and attain pure minds, pure beings such as Buddhas will definitely appear clearly to us.

Jewel Lotus Great Subduer

If we strive to attain higher realizations before we have mastered the basics, we must expect to become discouraged. We need to understand that even the highest realizations have small beginnings and learn to value the small experiences of Dharma that we have already achieved. Perhaps our attitude towards other people is less biased than it used to be, perhaps we are more patient or less arrogant, or perhaps our faith is stronger. These small improvements are the seeds that will eventually grow into higher realizations, and we should cherish them accordingly. We should not expect great changes straight away. We all have Buddha nature,[36] and now that we have met perfect instructions on the path to enlightenment if we practise steadily, without becoming discouraged, eventually we will definitely achieve full enlightenment without having to undergo great hardships. So what reason is there to become discouraged?

There are three types of effort: armour-like effort, which is a strong determination to succeed that we generate at the beginning of a virtuous action; the effort of gathering virtuous Dharmas, which is the actual effort we apply when we strive to gain Dharma realizations; and the effort of benefiting others, which is the effort we apply when we strive to benefit other living beings.

We need to apply effort in a skilful way. Some people begin their practice with great enthusiasm like a waterfall caused by a sudden storm, cascading furiously for a short time and then trickling away to nothing when great results do not appear. Our effort should not be like this. At the very beginning of our practice we should make a firm decision that we will persevere until we achieve Buddhahood no matter how long it takes, even if it takes many lifetimes. Then we should practise gently and consistently, like a great river that flows day and night, year after year.

When we are tired we should relax and resume our effort when we are properly rested. If we try to force ourselves beyond our natural capacity we will only become tense, irritable, or sick. Dharma practice should be a joyful affair. If others see us miserable while we are practising Dharma they will not believe that Dharma brings peace and happiness. It is said that when we practise Dharma we should be like a child at play. When children are engrossed in their games, they feel completely contented and nothing can distract them.

The perfection of mental stabilization

Mental stabilization, or concentration, is a mind whose nature is to be single-pointedly placed on a virtuous object, and whose function is to prevent distraction. Any concentration motivated by bodhichitta is a perfection of mental stabilization.

For ordinary beings, concentration functions mainly by means of mental consciousness. Our sense consciousnesses can behold and remain single-pointedly on their objects, but these are not concentrations. For example, when our eye consciousness stares single-pointedly at a candle, or our ear consciousness becomes absorbed in a piece of music, we are not practising concentration. To improve our concentration so that we achieve the nine mental abidings and eventually tranquil abiding,[37] it is necessary for our mind to gather within and dwell upon its object single-pointedly. To achieve this, we must take as our main object of concentration a generic image[38] that appears to the mental consciousness. Eventually, through the power of concentration, the generic image is worn away and the object is perceived directly.

When the sea is rough, sediment is churned up and the water becomes murky, but when the wind dies down the mud gradually settles and the water becomes clear. Likewise, in a mind stilled by concentration, delusions subside and the mind becomes extremely lucid. At the moment our minds are intractable, refusing to cooperate with our virtuous intentions, but concentration melts the tension in our body and mind and makes them supple, comfortable, and easy to work with. It is difficult for a distracted mind to become sufficiently acquainted with its object to induce spontaneous realizations[39] because it feels as if the mind is 'here' and the object 'there'. A concentrated mind, however, enters into its object and mixes with it and, as a result, realizations of the stages of the path are quickly achieved.

Mental stabilization can be used for either mundane or supramundane purposes. The highest planes within cyclic existence are entered by refining the mind through the practice of concentration. After achieving tranquil abiding the meditator contemplates the gross and painful nature of the desire realm and the relative peace, purity, and subtlety of the form realm. Gradually he abandons the delusions pertaining to the desire realm – principally sensual desire and all forms of anger – and thereby becomes a god of the form realm. Continuing to refine his mind, he is able to ascend to progressively more subtle levels of existence, until he reaches the peak of cyclic existence, the highest level of the formless realm[40] which some non-Buddhists mistake for liberation. This is the highest state that can be achieved through concentration alone. Although at this stage all but the most subtle forms of delusion have been suppressed, self-grasping, the root of samsara, still has not been eliminated and so eventually the grosser delusions will arise and once again the meditator will have to descend to lower states. Only a direct realization of emptiness has the power to cut the continuum of self-grasping. Therefore, from the beginning we should be motivated by renunciation and bodhichitta to attain tranquil abiding so that we can overcome self-grasping and free ourselves and all other living beings from the sufferings of samsara.

In earlier times it was fairly easy to achieve tranquil abiding and the form and formless absorptions, but nowadays, as our merit decreases, our delusions grow stronger, and distractions abound, these attainments are much more difficult. Therefore we need to prepare well, especially by overcoming desirous attachment, and then be willing to practise steadily for a long time before we can achieve higher levels of concentration.

In the course of mastering the concentrations of the form and formless realms we achieve clairvoyance and other miracle powers. Although these have little meaning in themselves, they can be used by Bodhisattvas to enhance their ability to help others. For example, although we may have very good intentions, sometimes, through not knowing others' minds, we misjudge a situation and our actions prove to be more of a hindrance than a help. Such problems can be overcome by developing a clairvoyance that knows others' minds. However, we should not strive to attain clairvoyance, or any other miracle power, simply for our own sake. If we have taken Bodhisattva vows, we should have a strong interest in improving our concentration as a means of fulfilling our wish to benefit others. If, having taken Bodhisattva vows, we show no interest in improving our concentration we incur a secondary downfall.

The perfection of wisdom

Wisdom is a virtuous mind that functions mainly to dispel doubt and confusion by understanding its object thoroughly. Wisdom that is motivated by bodhichitta is a perfection of wisdom.

Wisdom is not worldly intelligence. It is possible to have great intelligence but little wisdom. For example, people who invent weapons of mass destruction are very clever from a worldly point of view, but they have very little wisdom. Similarly, there are people who know a great many facts and understand complex technical subjects, but have no idea how to maintain a peaceful mind and lead a virtuous way of life. Such people may have great intelligence, but they have little wisdom.

Wisdom is a special type of understanding that induces peace of mind by clearly distinguishing what is virtuous and to be practised, from what is non-virtuous and to be avoided. Wisdom provides our spiritual practice with vision. Without the guidance of wisdom the other five perfections would be blind and would not be able to lead us to the final destination of Buddhahood.

A direct realization of emptiness, the ultimate nature of reality, can be achieved only by a wisdom that is conjoined with tranquil abiding. With a wavering mind we will never perceive a subtle object such as emptiness clearly enough to be able to realize it directly, just as we cannot read a book by the light of a flickering candle. Training in meditative stabilization is like shielding our mind from the winds of distracting thoughts, while wisdom is like the light of the flame itself. When these two factors are brought together, we achieve a clear and powerful perception of the object.

After achieving tranquil abiding we should strive to attain a union of tranquil abiding and superior seeing observing emptiness. The nature of superior seeing is wisdom. Just as tranquil abiding is a special and superior kind of concentration, so superior seeing is a superior wisdom arising in dependence upon tranquil abiding. When we have attained tranquil abiding our concentration cannot be disturbed by conceptual thoughts. It is unshakeable like a huge mountain that cannot be moved by the wind. With such stable concentration we can investigate our observed object more thoroughly. Through the power of repeated investigation, we will eventually gain a superior knowledge or insight into the nature of our object of meditation. This wisdom of investigation induces a special suppleness. Wisdom that is

King of Mount Meru

qualified by such suppleness is superior seeing. When we first attain superior seeing observing emptiness our realization of emptiness is still conceptual, but by continuing to meditate on emptiness with the wisdom of superior seeing we can gradually eliminate the generic image until finally we perceive emptiness directly, without even a trace of conceptuality.

Since Bodhisattvas wish to become enlightened as soon as possible they have a strong wish to accumulate powerful merit quickly. Therefore they practise each of the six perfections in conjunction with all the others. For example, when Bodhisattvas practise giving they do so without self-interest, expecting nothing in return. In this way they practise in accordance with their Bodhisattva vows and combine the perfection of giving with the perfection of moral discipline. By patiently accepting any hardships involved and not allowing anger to arise if no gratitude is shown, they combine the perfection of giving with the perfection of patience. By giving joyfully they combine the perfection of giving with the perfection of effort; and by concentrating their minds, thinking: 'May the merit of my action of giving enable this person to attain Buddhahood', they combine it with the perfection of mental stabilization. Finally, by realizing that the giver, the gift, and the action of giving all lack inherent existence, they combine the perfection of giving with the perfection of wisdom.

The other perfections can also be practised in this way, with each perfection being practised in conjunction with all the others. This is the armour-like skilful action of a Bodhisattva that hastens the completion of the two accumulations of merit and wisdom. Because Bodhisattvas perform all their actions with the motivation of bodhichitta their whole life is taken up with the practice of the six perfections and in this way they avoid committing any of the root and secondary downfalls of the Bodhisattva vows.

The Results

By practising the methods described in this book we will eventually achieve spontaneous bodhichitta, and from then on the wish to attain Buddhahood for the sake of all sentient beings will arise naturally day and night. At this point we will become a Bodhisattva on the Mahayana path of accumulation.

When, by continuing to train in concentration and wisdom with bodhichitta motivation, we achieve a union of tranquil abiding and superior seeing observing emptiness, we become a Bodhisattva on the Mahayana path of preparation, and when by improving this union we gain a direct realization of emptiness, we advance to the Mahayana path of seeing. At this stage we abandon all intellectually-formed delusions. Then, when we achieve an uncontaminated wisdom that acts as a direct antidote to the first level of innate delusions, we advance to the Mahayana path of meditation.

By continuing to meditate on emptiness, eventually we will attain the vajra-like concentration of the path of meditation, which is the direct antidote to the most subtle obstructions to omniscience and the last moment of the mind of a sentient being. In the next moment we attain the Mahayana Path of No More Learning and become a fully enlightened Buddha. Then our mind will be free from all obstructions, we shall see all past, present, and future phenomena directly and simultaneously, and we shall have the ability to help all sentient beings by emanating infinite Emanation Bodies.

Dedication

We should pray:

> Through the virtues I have created by reading, contemplating, and meditating on these instructions, may all living beings enter into the Bodhisattva's way of life and swiftly accomplish the supreme bliss of full enlightenment.

Appendix I
Condensed Meaning of the Text

The commentary to The Bodhisattva Vow *has five parts:*

1 Introduction
2 The method for receiving and maintaining the Bodhisattva vows
3 The method for completing the vows and trainings of a Bodhisattva
4 The results
5 Dedication

The method for receiving and maintaining the Bodhisattva vows has five parts:

1 Taking refuge vows
2 Generating bodhichitta
3 Maintaining aspiring bodhichitta by means of ritual
4 Taking the Bodhisattva vows
5 Maintaining joy and conscientiousness

The method for completing the vows and trainings of a Bodhisattva has three parts:

1 An explanation of the downfalls of the Bodhisattva vows
2 A method for purifying downfalls
3 The actual trainings of a Bodhisattva

An explanation of the downfalls of the Bodhisattva vows has two parts:

1 The forty-six secondary downfalls
2 The eighteen root downfalls

A method for purifying downfalls has two parts:

1 *The Mahayana Sutra of the Three Superior Heaps*
2 An explanation of the practice

An explanation of the practice has three parts:

1 An introduction to the practice
2 The visualization
3 The actual practice

The actual practice has three parts:

1 Purifying non-virtuous actions
2 Dedicating virtue
3 Conclusion

Purifying non-virtuous actions has four parts:

1 The power of reliance
2 The power of the antidote
3 The power of regret
4 The power of promise

The actual trainings of a Bodhisattva has six parts:

1 The perfection of giving
2 The perfection of moral discipline
3 The perfection of patience
4 The perfection of effort
5 The perfection of mental stabilization
6 The perfection of wisdom

The perfection of giving has three parts:

1 Giving material things
2 Giving Dharma
3 Giving fearlessness

The perfection of moral discipline has three parts:

1 The moral discipline of restraint
2 The moral discipline of gathering virtuous Dharmas
3 The moral discipline of benefiting living beings

The perfection of patience has three parts:

1 The patience of not retaliating
2 The patience of voluntarily enduring suffering
3 The patience of definitely thinking about Dharma

Appendix II
Vows and Commitments

_____

THE REFUGE VOWS

1 Not to go for refuge in teachers who contradict Buddha's view, or in samsaric gods.
2 To regard any image of Buddha as an actual Buddha.
3 Not to harm others.
4 To regard all Dharma scriptures as the actual Dharma Jewel.
5 Not to allow ourselves to be influenced by people who reject Buddha's teaching.
6 To regard anyone who wears the robes of an ordained person as an actual Sangha Jewel.
7 To go for refuge to the Three Jewels again and again, remembering their good qualities and the differences between them.
8 To offer the first portion of whatever we eat and drink to the Three Jewels, remembering their kindness.
9 With compassion, always to encourage others to go for refuge.
10 Remembering the benefits of going for refuge, to go for refuge at least three times during the day and three times during the night.
11 To perform every action with complete trust in the Three Jewels.
12 Never to forsake the Three Jewels even at the cost of our life, or as a joke.

THE PRECEPTS OF ASPIRING BODHICHITTA

1 To remember the benefits of bodhichitta six times a day.
2 To generate bodhichitta six times a day.
3 Not to abandon any living being.
4 To accumulate merit and wisdom.
5 Not to cheat or deceive our Preceptors[41] or Spiritual Guides.
6 Not to criticize those who have entered the Mahayana.
7 Not to cause others to regret their wholesome actions.
8 Not to pretend to have good qualities or hide our faults without a special, pure intention.

THE ROOT DOWNFALLS OF THE BODHISATTVA VOWS

1 Praising ourself and scorning others.
2 Not giving wealth or Dharma.
3 Not accepting others' apologies.
4 Abandoning the Mahayana.
5 Stealing the property of the Three Jewels.
6 Abandoning Dharma.
7 Taking away saffron robes.
8 Committing the five heinous actions.
9 Holding wrong views.
10 Destroying places such as towns.
11 Explaining emptiness to those who are likely to misunderstand.
12 Causing others to abandon the Mahayana.
13 Causing others to abandon the Pratimoksha.
14 Belittling the Hinayana.
15 Speaking falsely about profound emptiness.
16 Accepting property that has been stolen from the Three Jewels.
17 Making bad rules.
18 Giving up bodhichitta.

THE SECONDARY DOWNFALLS OF THE
BODHISATTVA VOWS

1 Not making offerings to the Three Jewels every day.
2 Indulging in worldly pleasures out of attachment.
3 Being disrespectful to those who received Bodhisattva vows before us.
4 Not replying to others.
5 Not accepting invitations.
6 Not accepting gifts.
7 Not giving Dharma to those who desire it.
8 Forsaking those who have broken their moral discipline.
9 Not acting in ways that cause others to generate faith.
10 Doing little to benefit others.
11 Not believing that Bodhisattvas' compassion ensures that all their actions are pure.
12 Acquiring wealth or fame through wrong livelihood.
13 Indulging in frivolity.
14 Claiming that Bodhisattvas need not abandon samsara.
15 Not avoiding a bad reputation.
16 Not helping others to avoid negativity.
17 Retaliating to harm or abuse.
18 Not apologizing when we have the opportunity.
19 Not accepting others' apologies.
20 Making no effort to control our anger.
21 Gathering a circle of followers out of desire for profit or respect.
22 Not trying to overcome laziness.
23 Indulging in senseless conversation out of attachment.
24 Neglecting to train in mental stabilization.
25 Not overcoming obstacles to mental stabilization.
26 Being preoccupied with the taste of mental stabilization.
27 Abandoning the Hinayana.
28 Studying the Hinayana to the detriment of our Mahayana practice.
29 Studying non-Dharma subjects without a good reason.

30 Becoming engrossed in non-Dharma subjects for their own sake.
31 Criticizing other Mahayana traditions.
32 Praising ourself and scorning others.
33 Making no effort to study Dharma.
34 Preferring to rely on books rather than on our Spiritual Guide.
35 Not going to the assistance of those in need.
36 Neglecting to take care of the sick.
37 Not acting to dispel suffering.
38 Not helping others to overcome their bad habits.
39 Not returning help to those who benefit us.
40 Not relieving the distress of others.
41 Not giving to those who seek charity.
42 Not taking special care of disciples.
43 Not acting in accordance with the inclinations of others.
44 Not praising the good qualities of others.
45 Not doing wrathful actions when appropriate.
46 Not using miracle powers, threatening actions, and so forth.

Notes

1 There are two main paths, or vehicles, in Buddhism – the Hinayana Path and the Mahayana Path. The former emphasizes the attainment of liberation for oneself alone, and the latter emphasizes the attainment of enlightenment, or Buddhahood, for the sake of others.

2 The actions listed here are the ten non-virtuous actions, which should be avoided at all costs. The first three actions – killing, stealing, and sexual misconduct – are non-virtuous actions of body; the next four – lying, divisive speech, hurtful speech, and idle gossip – are non-virtuous actions of speech; and the last three – covetousness, malice, and holding wrong views – are non-virtuous actions of mind.

3 Tantric bodhichitta is a wish to attain enlightenment as a Tantric Buddha right away in order to rescue sentient beings from samsara as quickly as possible.

4 In the *Vinaya Sutras*, Buddha mainly explained the practice of moral discipline, and in particular the Pratimoksha moral discipline.

5 Lamrim, or the Stages of the Path, is a systematic presentation of all the stages of the path to enlightenment.

6 According to Tantra, the two main obstacles to be overcome are ordinary appearances and ordinary conceptions. These are overcome by training in the two stages of Tantra: generation stage and completion stage.

7 Merit, or good fortune, is the positive energy that results from virtuous actions. We need to accumulate a vast collection of merit in order to attain enlightenment.

8 The Three Jewels are the three objects of refuge: the Buddha Jewel, the Dharma Jewel, and the Sangha Jewel. They are called 'Jewels' because they are both rare and precious.

9 Bodhisattvas are sometimes referred to as 'Sons' or 'Daughters' of the Buddhas. The analogy is with sons and daughters of monarchs. Just as a prince or a princess is destined to become a monarch, so a Bodhisattva is destined to become a Buddha.

10 Hearers and Solitary Conquerors are types of Hinayana practitioner. Solitary Conquerors are superior to Hearers from the point of view of both merit and wisdom, but in many respects they are are inferior to Buddhas.

11 A Bodhisattva seeks to abandon not only cyclic existence but also a Hinayana nirvana, or solitary peace.

12 'Sugata' is another term for a Buddha. It indicates that Buddhas have attained a state of immaculate and indestructible bliss.

13 Self-cherishing is a mental attitude that considers oneself to be precious or important. It is regarded as a principal object to be abandoned by Mahayana practitioners.

14 Delusions are disturbing states of mind that destroy our inner peace and happiness. They are the principal object to be abandoned by those seeking liberation from samsara.

15 The vast path includes all the method practices from the initial cultivation of compassion through to the final attainment of the Form Body of a Buddha. The profound path includes all the wisdom practices that lead to a direct realization of emptiness and ultimately to the Truth Body of a Buddha.

16 Emptiness is lack of inherent existence, the ultimate nature of all phenomena.

17 Sense of shame is a virtuous mental factor that causes us to refrain from non-virtue for reasons that concern ourselves, and consideration for others is a virtuous mental factor that causes us to refrain from non-virtue for reasons that concern others.

18 Nalanda Monastery was a great Mahayana seat of learning and practice in ancient India.

19 Avalokiteshvara, or Chenrezig in Tibetan, is the embodiment of the compassion of all the Buddhas.

20 Buddha Kashyapa was the third Buddha to appear in this world and turn the Wheel of Dharma, the previous two being Buddha Kraccuchchanda and Buddha Kanakamuni.

Buddha Shakyamuni was the fourth Buddha, and Buddha Maitreya will be the fifth.

21 Vasubhandu was a great Buddhist scholar who was converted to the Mahayana by his brother, Asanga.

22 Buddha's two mudras symbolize that he has overcome the four maras or demons. The nectar in the bowl symbolizes triumph over the mara of death, the mara of the delusions, and the mara of the aggregates; and touching the ground with the right hand symbolizes triumph over the maras of Devaputra, misguided beings in the god realms who attempt to prevent authentic spiritual progress.

23 The thirty-two signs, sometimes called the 'major marks', such as the sign of the wheel on the palms of the hands and the soles of the feet, and the eighty indications, sometimes called the 'minor marks', such as copper-coloured nails, are special characteristics of a Buddha's form.

24 A Superior being is any being who has attained a direct realization of emptiness.

25 A Foe Destroyer, or Arhat in Sanskrit, is a practitioner who has abandoned all delusions and their seeds by training on the spiritual paths. In this context, the term 'foe' refers to the delusions.

26 Learner Superiors are Superior beings who are still training on the learning paths, that is, Superior beings on either the path of seeing or the path of meditation.

27 A Buddha has four bodies – the Wisdom Truth Body, the Nature Body, the Enjoyment Body, and the Emanation Bodies. The first is a Buddha's omniscient mind; the second is the emptiness or ultimate nature of his mind; the third is his actual Form Body, which is very subtle; and the fourth, of which each Buddha manifests a countless number, are gross Form Bodies that are visible to ordinary beings. The Wisdom Truth Body and the Nature Body are both included within the Truth Body, and the Enjoyment Body and the Emanation Bodies are both included within the Form Body.

28 There are two types of obstruction covering the minds of sentient beings: obstructions to liberation and obstructions to omniscience. The former are the delusions and their seeds. These have to be abandoned in order to

attain liberation. The latter are the imprints of the delusions that remain in the mind even after the delusions have been abandoned. These have to be abandoned in order to attain Buddhahood, or enlightenment.

29 Here, the clear light of bliss refers to a perfectly pure subtle mind and the illusory body refers to a perfectly pure subtle body, both of which are attained by completing the stages of Secret Mantra, or Tantra.

30 Pujas are ceremonies in which offerings and other acts of devotion are performed in front of holy beings.

31 There are eight unfree states into which we can be reborn. They are: rebirth as a hell being, rebirth as a hungry spirit, rebirth as an animal, rebirth as an ordinary god, rebirth in a country where there is no religion, rebirth where there is no Buddhadharma, rebirth with mental or physical disability, and rebirth as one who holds wrong views denying Dharma. They are called 'unfree' states because they allow no freedom for spiritual practice.

32 The four ways of gathering disciples practised by Bodhisattvas are: pleasing others by giving them material gifts or whatever they need, teaching Dharma to lead others to liberation, helping others in their Dharma practice by giving them encouragement, and showing them a good example by always practising what we teach.

33 Geshe Langri Tangpa was one of the great Kadampa Geshes. He composed *Eight Verses of Training the Mind*.

34 Mundane happiness is the limited happiness that can be found within cyclic existence, such as the happiness of humans and gods. Supramundane happiness is the pure happiness of liberation and enlightenment.

35 Meditation on our precious human rebirth and meditation on death and impermanence are included within the cycle of Lamrim meditations. They are explained in *Joyful Path of Good Fortune* and *A Meditation Handbook*.

36 Our Buddha nature is our potential for enlightenment. All sentient beings without exception have the potential to become enlightened beings, but to realize this potential we must meet an authentic Mahayana Spiritual Guide and sincerely practise his or her instructions

37 When we train in improving our concentration we progress

through nine levels of concentration, known as 'the nine mental abidings', before we achieve actual tranquil abiding. Tranquil abiding is a concentration that possesses the special bliss of suppleness of body and mind that is attained in dependence upon completing the nine mental abidings. Instructions on how to train in tranquil abiding can be found in *Joyful Path of Good Fortune* and *Meaningful to Behold*.

38 The generic image of an object is the mental image of that object that appears to a conceptual mental consciousness. Even if the object itself is impermanent and changes moment by moment, the generic image of that object will be permanent, and not subject to momentary change.

39 When, through the power of familiarity, a realization arises naturally, without any effort, it has become a spontaneous realization.

40 There are three levels within cyclic existence: the desire realm, the form realm, and the formless realm.

41 Preceptors are Spiritual Guides who give us vows or commitments to observe.

Bibliography

Geshe Kelsang Gyatso is a highly respected meditation master and scholar of the Mahayana Buddhist tradition founded by Je Tsongkhapa. Since arriving in the UK in 1977, Geshe Kelsang has worked tirelessly to establish pure Buddhadharma in the West. Over this period he has given extensive teachings on the major scriptures of the Mahayana. These teachings are currently being published and will provide a comprehensive presentation of the essential Sutra and Tantra practices of Mahayana Buddhism.

Books in print

Buddhism in the Tibetan Tradition: A Guide. An introduction to Tibetan Buddhism. (Penguin, 1990.)

Clear Light of Bliss. Mahamudra in Vajrayana Buddhism. (2nd. edn. Tharpa, 1991.)

Guide to Dakini Land. A commentary to the Highest Yoga Tantra practice of Venerable Vajrayogini. (Tharpa, 1991.)

Heart Jewel. A commentary to the *Heart Jewel* sadhana, the essential practice of the New Kadam Tradition of Mahayana Buddhism. (Tharpa, 1991.)

Heart of Wisdom. A commentary to the *Heart Sutra*. (3rd. edn. Tharpa, 1990.)

Joyful Path of Good Fortune. The stages of the path to enlightenment. (Tharpa, 1990.)

Meaningful to Behold. A commentary to Shantideva's *Guide to the Bodhisattva's Way of Life.* (3rd. edn. Tharpa, 1990.)

A Meditation Handbook. A practical guide to Buddhist meditation. (Tharpa, 1990.)

Universal Compassion. A commentary to Bodhisattva Chekhawa's *Training the Mind in Seven Points.* (Tharpa, 1988.)

Forthcoming books

Great Treasury of Merit. A commentary to *Offering to the Spiritual Guide (Lama Chöpa).*

Types of Mind. An explanation of the nature, types, and functions of mind.

Ocean of Nectar. A commentary to Chandrakirti's *Guide to the Middle Way.*

Great Mother of the Conquerors. A commentary to the *Perfection of Wisdom Sutras.*

Tantric Grounds and Paths. An explanation of the grounds and paths of the four classes of Tantra.

Going for Refuge. An introduction to the practice of Buddhist refuge.

Essence of the Vajrayana. A commentary to the Highest Yoga Tantra practice of Glorious Heruka.

Sadhanas

Geshe Kelsang is also supervising the translation of a collection of essential sadhanas. Those already in print include:

The Bodhisattva's Confession of Moral Downfalls. The purification practice of the *Mahayana Sutra of the Three Superior Heaps.*

Chenrezig Sadhana. Prayers and requests to the Buddha of compassion.

Dakini Yoga: Vajrayogini Six-Session Sadhana. Six-session Guru Yoga combined with self-generation as Vajrayogini.

Essence of Good Fortune. Prayers for the six preparatory practices for meditation on the stages of the path to enlightenment.

Great Compassionate Mother. Praises and requests to the Twenty-one Taras combined with the practice of self-generation.

Great Mother. A method for averting obstacles in conjunction with the *Heart Sutra.*

Heart Jewel. The Guru Yoga of Je Tsongkhapa combined with the practice of his Dharma Protector.

Medicine Guru Sadhana. Prayers and requests to the Assembly
of Seven Medicine Buddhas.
Wishfulfilling Jewel. The Guru Yoga of Je Tsongkhapa
combined with the short sadhana of his Dharma Protector.

For a complete list of books and sadhanas by Geshe Kelsang
Gyatso please write to:

Tharpa Publications
15 Bendemeer Road
London SW15 1JX
England

Study Programmes

Geshe Kelsang has prepared three study programmes based on his books: the General Programme, the Foundation Programme, and the Teacher Training Programme. These are designed to fulfil the wishes of those who would like to study Buddhism systematically and thereby deepen their experience of the essential practices.

The General Programme provides a basic introduction to Buddhist view, meditation, and action, and various kinds of teaching and practice from both Sutra and Tantra.

The Foundation Programme is designed for those who prefer a more structured approach to their spiritual training. Based on five of Geshe Kelsang's books, this programme lasts for approximately three years. The classes consist of readings, teachings, discussion, pujas, and meditations. Each subject concludes with an examination.

The Teacher Training Programme is designed for those who wish to train as authentic Dharma Teachers. This programme, which takes seven years to complete, is based on eleven of Geshe Kelsang's books. To qualify as Dharma Teachers, participants must complete the study of all eleven texts, pass an examination in each subject, satisfy certain criteria with regard to life-style, and complete various meditation retreats.

In recent years, Geshe Kelsang has received many requests to found Centres where these programmes can be studied, and there are now a number of such Centres in the UK, Spain, the US, Canada, and Mexico.

The addresses for correspondence are given overleaf.

Manjushri Institute
Conishead Priory,
Ulverston,
Cumbria, UK.
Tel 0229-54029
Founded 1975

Madhyamaka Centre
Kilnwick Percy Hall,
Pocklington, York, UK.
Tel 0759-304832
Founded 1979

Vajravarahi Centre
38 Deepdale Road,
Preston,
Lancs, UK.
Tel 0772-59094
Founded 1980

Instituto Dharma
Notario Quintana 42,
Ciutadella 07760,
Menorca, Spain.
Tel 971-385756
Founded 1981

Tara Centre
4 Manchester Road,
Buxton, Derbyshire, UK.
Tel 0298-72026
Founded 1983

Chenrezig Centre
21 Portland St,
Lancaster, Lancs, UK.
Tel 0524-68437
Founded 1984

Amitayus Centre
'Blakelow',
Newcastle Road,
Nantwich, Cheshire, UK.
Tel 0270-662156
Founded 1985

Losang Dragpa Centre
7 Branwell Drive, Haworth,
Keighley, W.Yorks, UK.
Tel 0535-642815
Founded 1985

Khedrubje Centre
'Cotswold',
Chantry Way, Swanland,
N. Humberside, UK.
Tel 0482-631744
Founded 1985

**York Mahayana
Buddhist Centre**
Osbourne House, School Lane,
Fulford, York, UK.
Tel 0904-621508
Founded 1986

Gyaltsabje Centre
106 Penrhyn Road
Sheffield, S. Yorks, UK.
Tel 0742-682359
Founded 1986

Asociacion Vajradharma
Apartado 161,
Cordoba,
Spain.
Founded 1986

**Huddersfield Mahayana
Buddhist Centre**
11 Sunnybank, Denby Dale,
Nr. Huddersfield,
W. Yorks, UK.
Tel 0484-865007
Founded 1988

**Teesside Mahayana
Buddhist Centre**
7 Minster Walk,
Hurworth, Darlington,
Co. Durham, UK.
Tel 0325-720124
Founded 1988

**Nottingham Mahayana
Buddhist Centre**
5b Tennyson Street,
Nottingham, NG7 4FT,
UK.
Tel 0602-625158
Founded 1989

**Buddhist Institute
California**
13742 Orleans Court,
Saratoga, CA 95070, USA.
Tel 408-867-4616
Founded 1990

**Buddhist Institute
San Francisco**
3040 Jackson Street,
San Francisco,
CA 94115, USA.
Tel 415-673-5049
Founded 1990

**Buddhist Institute
Toronto**
1172 Mount Pleasant Road
Toronto, M4N 2T2,
Canada.
Tel 416-488-5554
Founded 1990

Instituto Budista Mexico
Calle Independicia 124,
San Antonio,
Tlycapan, CP41915,
Chapala, Jalisco, Mexico.
Tel 52-376-54188
Founded 1990

**Leeds Mahayana
Buddhist Centre**
3 Roman Drive,
Leeds, LS8 2DR,
UK.
Tel 0532-654634
Founded 1991

Heruka Centre
P.O. Box 84,
London,
SW15 1JQ,
UK.
Founded 1991

**Manchester Mahayana
Buddhist Centre**
c/o Tara Centre,
4 Manchester Road,
Buxton, Derbyshire, UK.
Tel 0298-72026
Founded 1991

Index